ioti
foll
(Tel
(3952
Two

You
that

WITHDRAWN AND SOLD
BY
STAFFORDSHIRE
COUNTY LIBRARY

Fenland Railwayman

Fenland Railwayman

Arthur Randell

Edited by Enid Porter
Curator of the Cambridge and County Folk Museum

Designed and illustrated by Andrew Young

Routledge & Kegan Paul London

---

great change from farming; in fact, in those first few weeks I thought several times of going back to the land, but decided to give things a good trial.

Station-masters in those days were provided with free coal and oil, so when the coal trucks arrived with supplies for the fires in the office, waiting-room, signal-box and porters' room, one of my jobs in my first days at work was to see that Mr Paige's coal shed was kept filled and that he had plenty of oil.

Our burning oil used to come from Stratford in 40-gallon casks, five at a time, and these had to be hoisted on to trestles ready for tapping. Our hand-lamps burned rape oil – greasy stuff but good for several other things besides burning. Nearly everyone had oil-burning lamps on their bicycles so a good many people from near the station used to come along with the request: 'Can I borrow a drop of oil for my bicycle?'

One old man, who was officially a roadman but did a good deal of poaching as a sideline, used to come up to me with a medicine bottle in his hand and whisper: 'Ha' yer got a drop of oil for us?' If anybody was about he would hide the bottle and talk of anything else but oil till the coast was clear, then, when I'd filled his bottle he would whisper: 'There's a long-tailed 'un outside,' by which I knew he had brought a pheasant along for me.

A good many pig-keepers, too, used to come for a drop of oil because it was excellent for killing the lice which often get behind pigs' ears. Rape oil was also good for cleaning bicycles and garden tools as it prevented them from rusting, so altogether the station was a popular place when our supplies of oil came in.

After I had been at my new job for a few weeks I began to enjoy meeting the trains from London, March and Peterborough and helping to load on to them a wide assortment of goods – milk, fish, fruit, sausages and mail. I had three mates working with me – one an old school chum – and they were extremely helpful, showing me what to do and always willing to stay on a bit later

First Published 1968
by Routledge & Kegan Paul Limited
Broadway House, 68–74 Carter Lane
London, E.C.4

Printed in Great Britain by
Cox & Wyman Ltd.
London, Fakenham and Reading
© Arthur Randell 1968

No part of this book may be reproduced
in any form without permission from
the publisher, except for the quotation
of brief passages in criticism

SBN 7100 6152 8

Contents

Foreword   vii

First Days on the Railway   1

At Magdalen Road   11

More Memories of Magdalen Road   23

At Coldham   37

Waldersea Siding   45

The Decline of Waldersea   53

Whitemoor Marshalling Yards and Old Steam Eng

War and Accidents   73

Some Personal Opinions and Last Memories   83

Fenland Railwayman

Arthur Randell

Edited by Enid Porter
Curator of the Cambridge and County Folk Museum

Designed and illustrated by Andrew Young

Routledge & Kegan Paul London

*First Published 1968
by Routledge & Kegan Paul Limited
Broadway House, 68–74 Carter Lane
London, E.C.4*

*Printed in Great Britain by
Cox & Wyman Ltd.
London, Fakenham and Reading
© Arthur Randell 1968*

*No part of this book may be reproduced
in any form without permission from
the publisher, except for the quotation
of brief passages in criticism*

SBN 7100 6152 8

Contents

Foreword   vii

First Days on the Railway   1

At Magdalen Road   11

More Memories of Magdalen Road   23

At Coldham   37

Waldersea Siding   45

The Decline of Waldersea   53

Whitemoor Marshalling Yards and Old Steam Engines   61

War and Accidents   73

Some Personal Opinions and Last Memories   83

Foreword

In the archives of the British Broadcasting Corporation is a recording of the sounds of an unidentified country railway station: the chirruping of birds, the crowing of a cock, the bleating of sheep and the lowing of cattle from the vans of a passing goods train, the metallic ring of milk churns as they are lifted from trucks on to the platform. A steam train puffs lazily in and comes to a stop; there is the noise of passengers descending; doors are slammed, the guard blows his whistle and away the train moves to stop, probably, at a similar station only a few miles down the line. Arthur Randell, in this little book, writes of his life and work on stations in Norfolk and Cambridgeshire not very different from this.

While many of us who have grown up in the age of steam engines secretly regret the passing of the huge monsters which, at main-line termini stood impatiently waiting to pull out express trains, sending up, meanwhile, to the grimy station roof great billows of steam which descended like a fine Scotch mist, it is perhaps the slow journeys on branch lines which we best remember from childhood. The leisurely speed of the train, the frequent stops may have been exasperating to our elders, but what an opportunity they gave to observe the passing countryside and the activity on small rural stations.

Many of these stations are now closed and derelict; some – and Sandy in Bedfordshire springs immediately to mind – are still in use to remind us of what a pleasant picture they presented. Flowers grew on banks against the fences, framing the name of the station set out in whitewashed stones against a background of the Station-master's runner beans; the paintwork of waiting-rooms and ticket offices gleamed in the colours of the old private railway companies; a whistle-blowing guard set the train in motion with a majestic wave of his flag, and porters laid the dust on the platforms with water sprinkled from a can in intricate whorls and circles.

At each stop crates of protesting fowls were placed in or removed from the guard's van; passengers on their way to or from near-by market towns entered or alighted and there was village gossip in the compartments and critical comment of the crops in the fields alongside the line, while at numerous sidings were iron-railed pens full of livestock awaiting the arrival of the next goods train. Arthur Randell has driven into and out of trucks many ancestors of the sheep and cattle which now peer down on us in towns through the slatted sides of tiered, motor-driven lorries; he has hoisted into railway vans countless bales of hay such as, today, bring a reminder of the countryside as they are driven through our streets; and he has loaded vast quantities of the rich-smelling strawberries from Friday Bridge and Wisbech which once formed so important and valuable a part of railway freight. Many hours he has spent, too, working the signals in his box at Coldham and Waldersea looking out over the flat, fenland fields.

In company with other railwaymen of his generation he regrets the passing of much that was part of his daily life: the horses which brought the farm produce to the stations; the bustle and excitement of the fruit season; the regular meetings with farmers, market gardeners and landowners who used the railway for loading and for travel; the jostling crowds on country stations who journeyed regularly to King's Lynn, Wisbech, March and Peterborough. He has his own views on why the railways have lost so much trade and does not hesitate to express them or to suggest how the decline might perhaps have been halted.

Though never a driver he still has a great admiration for the old steam engines and for the men who drove them and who, as he tells us, tended and treated them as though they were living friends. To him work on a country station was never dull and he has many anecdotes to tell of the Fenland characters who worked with him on the railway, who visited the stations and travelled on the trains or shared his hut at night.

Chances of promotion came his way but he would never take them, for they would probably have meant his leaving his native Fens. At Magdalen Road, at Coldham and finally at Waldersea Siding, where he still lives near the signal-box which he manned for so many years, he was able to do work that he enjoyed in surroundings that he loved for Arthur Randell is, above all, that most enviable, perhaps, of all people in the world today – a happy and contented countryman.

Enid Porter

Early Days

First Days on the Railway

I shall always remember July 19th, 1918, as the day on which I gave up farm work and mole-catching and went to work on the old Great Eastern Railway. I left Magdalen Road, the station for my Norfolk village of Wiggenhall St Mary Magdalen, at seven o'clock in the morning to travel to Cambridge. It was the first time I had ever been in a train without my parents, and that was only to King's Lynn or, once a year, to Hunstanton.

When I arrived in Cambridge I was told to report to an office next to the station where I found about twenty-five lads of my own age and a dozen or so young women. Most of these, says Arthur Randell, were to be trained as signalwomen, many railwaymen being on active service. After we had handed over our birth certificates and the other papers we had been asked to bring, we were taken up in pairs to a kind of cat-walk high above the station to have our eyes tested.

The Inspector made us walk along until he shouted 'Stop!', at which we had to turn round and tell him what letter of the alphabet he was holding in his hand. He made quite a game of the whole business, for every now and then he would hold up a letter – especially one that could be confused with another – upside down to see if we really could tell the difference between, say, an A and a V.

After this he had us picking up coloured pieces of wool from a big heap jumbled up on a table.

'Pick out all the red pieces,' he said, and when he thought we had done so he shuffled all the pieces together and, adding to them the length of wool which he had hidden up his sleeve, said jokingly: 'What about this bit?'

As all this sight-testing went on in full view of people on the platform you can guess that we got quite a lot of laughs from them and a good deal of friendly advice.

After the tests were over we were sent to a doctor whose surgery was on Newmarket Road, but when we got there we were told that he was out on his rounds and would not be back until half past two. When we returned in the afternoon some of us nearly got sent home without being examined, because two or three of the lads kept laughing and joking as we waited, till the doctor threatened:

'Any more noise and you can all go back until tomorrow.'

This quietened them and we were all duly examined and passed as fit – probably, I think, because we were all breathing – and told to report back to the station.

There, after another wait, this time for the office staff to come back from their tea-break, we were fitted out with our railway caps and arm-bands. The cap given to me, with its big brass letters G E R on the front, was so large that only my ears kept it from falling over my eyes.

Then we had to meet the District Superintendent who looked, in his dark suit and glasses, more like a chapel parson than a railway official. He spoke to us in a friendly way, telling us to do our best and we would find everything went well. More advice was given us by an Inspector Rose, whom I was to meet several times later. He it was who, when I was passed out for signal duty, told me: 'Remember this, you can always answer a delay better than you can an accident,' a piece of advice which I never forgot and always acted upon.

After we had signed a few papers and filled in membership forms for the Sick and Orphans' Society we were dismissed to catch the last train home in an hour's time. The train was crowded and, as it was wartime, many of the regular staff were in the Forces. No one, therefore, told me and another lad who was travelling with me, that we should change at Ely. The realization that we were in the wrong portion of the train came when some soldiers in the compartment mentioned that they were going to Norwich. So we got out at Shippea Hill and stood there like a couple of lost lambs until the Station-master looked up the time-table for us and found that, by catching the 9.30 p.m. back to Ely we could get home on the Mail train just before midnight by way of March and Wisbech. So I did not get back to Magdalen Road until two o'clock in the morning.

At nine o'clock on the following Monday morning I reported for work at Magdalen Road where I was introduced to the Stationmaster, Mr Paige – a big man and very smart with his clipped beard, long-tailed jacket and stiff white collar which turned down at the corners.

At that time Magdalen Road was a very busy station. It lies six miles from King's Lynn, five from Downham on the main double line, and nine from Wisbech on the single or branch line. My first job was to help to collect up all the lamps, clean them and fill them with oil. The signal lamps were cleaned once a week, those used on the crossing-gate and in the office and waiting-room once a day. When that was finished I had to help tidy the platform and load the barrows ready for the passenger trains. It was not until I had been there a few days that I was allowed to meet the goods train or to help with the shunting. I found the work, at first, a great change from farming; in fact, in those first few weeks I thought several times of going back to the land, but decided to give things a good trial.

Station-masters in those days were provided with free coal and oil, so when the coal trucks arrived with supplies for the fires in the office, waiting-room, signal-box and porters' room, one of my jobs in my first days at work was to see that Mr Paige's coal shed was kept filled and that he had plenty of oil.

Our burning oil used to come from Stratford in 40-gallon casks, five at a time, and these had to be hoisted on to trestles ready for tapping. Our hand-lamps burned rape oil – greasy stuff but good for several other things besides burning. Nearly everyone had oil-burning lamps on their bicycles so a good many people from near the station used to come along with the request: 'Can I borrow a drop of oil for my bicycle?'

One old man, who was officially a roadman but did a good deal of poaching as a sideline, used to come up to me with a medicine bottle in his hand and whisper: 'Ha' yer got a drop of oil for us?' If anybody was about he would hide the bottle and talk of anything else but oil till the coast was clear, then, when I'd filled his bottle he would whisper: 'There's a long-tailed 'un outside,' by which I knew he had brought a pheasant along for me.

A good many pig-keepers, too, used to come for a drop of oil because it was excellent for killing the lice which often get behind pigs' ears. Rape oil was also good for cleaning bicycles and garden tools as it prevented them from rusting, so altogether the station was a popular place when our supplies of oil came in.

After I had been at my new job for a few weeks I began to enjoy meeting the trains from London, March and Peterborough and helping to load on to them a wide assortment of goods – milk, fish, fruit, sausages and mail. I had three mates working with me – one an old school chum – and they were extremely helpful, showing me what to do and always willing to stay on a bit later or to come a bit earlier if we all wanted to get off for a game of football.

One day, after I had been at the station for about a couple of months, I was called to the Station-master's office where I found him arranging an annual four days' leave with the old gateman, Woodhouse. I was told that, while he was on holiday, I was to look after the gates. Poor old Woodhouse, though, could not afford to go away for the whole time.

'We'll be off on Monday morning,' he said, 'and back Tuesday evening; then away again early on Wednesday till about five o'clock on Thursday.'

So I went on duty from nine o'clock on the Monday morning until eight o'clock on Tuesday evening when the old chap, although he was officially on leave, came to take over the gates until I replaced him on the next morning until the following evening. No overtime, I might add, was paid for this.

Immediately afterwards I was sent to look after some crossing-gates half-way between French Drove, on the March to Spalding Line, and Postland. I was to be on duty from eight o'clock in the morning until eight o'clock at night. It was very foggy when I got to French Drove and I had to grope my way for two miles along the line, and I had never been there before. After what seemed hours I saw a hut with the door open and a nice fire blazing away. The man whom I was relieving had thoughtfully left the door open otherwise I would never have seen the shelter hut in the fog but would have gone right past it.

I spent a week there and was then sent to Stanground, near Peterborough, to label coal trucks. One of the shunters there was a man named Alf Powell, and I can still remember how kind he was to me, helping to make things as easy as possible for I was travelling to and from Magdalen each day and so was putting in far more time than my normal twelve-hour shift.

One morning, just as my train was about to leave March, the

Station-master came running along the platform shouting out my name. I looked out of the window to see what he wanted and he told me to get out and catch the next train back to Magdalen Road because everyone there, except the Station-master, had gone down with influenza.

When I reached the station I found that a relief signalman, an old chap who was a french polisher by trade, had been sent for, and for a time he and the Station-master and I ran the whole place. It was the Spanish influenza that was raging and many people were dying of it. We managed to keep going for a bit until some of the staff returned, then I caught the complaint and had to stay away from work. I returned on November 11th, 1918, and was down near St German's Siding, two miles from Magdalen Road, when the news came that an Armistice had been signed and all the fighting was over.

In the following week I was sent to Wisbech Harbour where I stayed for eighteen weeks. Here my duties were shunting and point-turning. Every morning an engine would come down from Wisbech Goods drawing fifty to seventy trucks laden with coal, timber, potatoes, oranges and other goods. These were sorted out and placed either in English's Sidings (Messrs English Brothers, timber importers), the Gas Works Sidings or in Wilson's Manure Siding, while the remainder were pulled by horses into sidings where engines were not allowed to go.

Wisbech Harbour at that time was a very busy place and often the engine would have to make two trips, especially when goods had come in with Scotch seed potatoes or with timber from the Baltic. All the time I was working there the London Scottish Regiment was billeted in the timber shed of Messrs English Brothers, and every morning the pipers would be practising near to where we were shunting.

I worked with elderly engine drivers, members of 'The Old Men's Gang', which meant that they were always on day shifts and so never had to spend the night in lodgings. I have often wondered what they would have thought of today's diesel engines, for men such as these were proud of their steam engines and I have often seen one of them, after giving his engine a wipe with cotton waste, lean over and pat her affectionately, saying, 'You're a good old gal.'

The big factory now owned by Smedley's was being built near the harbour at that time. It was then owned by Keillers, the jam and marmalade manufacturers, and sometimes we had up to twenty or thirty trucks of oranges and lemons to deliver to their private sidings, and several loads of jam, mincemeat, marmalade and lemon curd to take away. Often there would be a few loose oranges in the trucks and Keiller's manager would bring us a few when he came into the office. Some of them were sweet enough, but others horribly bitter. I remember that one old man who was what country people call 'only ninepence to the shilling' used to come down to where we were working. All the drivers knew him and often gave him a copper or two – he did no proper work but lived on the few shillings a week allowed him by the workhouse – or a few oranges. But simple though he was, he knew the difference in the look of the two kinds of oranges, and if anyone offered him one of the bitter kind he got a good taste of the old chap's tongue.

What is now Clarkson's Hospital was a workhouse in 1918. A number of elderly and infirm people lived there permanently in addition to the tramps and roadsters who called for a free meal and a night's lodging which they had to pay for by an hour's work before they went on their way in the morning.

A big piece of land with pigsties on it belonged to the workhouse; it ran beside the harbour line. One siding near to it was always known as Workhouse Siding and another as Piggery Siding. Any inmates who were capable of work were sent down to this land to clean out and feed the pigs. Just before midday first one and then another of the old men would stroll up to the fence and ask us the time. At twelve o'clock the workhouse bell was tolled, and at the first stroke the men would be gone like rabbits, but it was a very different story when they all crawled back to work at one o'clock.

I enjoyed working down at the harbour. The men of the London Scottish were friendly chaps who used to give us pint mugs of tea and big slices of oat cake, and it was interesting to meet the foreign seamen off the timber ships. But all this is now in the past. Wisbech Harbour is no longer used by the railway and it is sad to think that the last train from there came up the single line only two years ago.

At Magdalen Road

One Saturday evening when I returned home from Wisbech Harbour by the late train, Mr Paige, the Magdalen Road Stationmaster met me and told me that I was to stay at the station regularly, starting at six o'clock on the Monday morning. The eight-hour day had just been introduced, so I was to make up the three shifts of eight hours each.

On the early shift I had to light the fires, attend to the first freight train which left King's Lynn at 5.45 a.m., load milk on to the London passenger train, barrow goods from the down to the up platform, attend to all the passenger trains and help with trans-shipping goods from the three other freight trains. Then there were lamps to be collected, cleaned and filled and help to be given to the goods porters in fastening ropes and tarpaulin sheets over the goods trucks. In fact there always seemed another job to be done as soon as one was finished.

On the second shift I worked from two o'clock in the afternoon until ten o'clock at night, attending to passenger trains, taking out the lamps when dusk fell, and loading barrows with milk and other goods ready for the evening train to London. Parcels had to be sorted out and, once the goods porters had gone home, there were always various freight trains from which empty horse boxes or cattle trucks had to be detached ready for loading next day.

The third shift, from ten o'clock at night until six in the morning, was usually quieter, though there were the up and down mail trains to be attended as well as several goods trains. Perhaps there might be five or six hundred sheep to be unloaded, or two or three hundred calves which had to be driven into W. Gotobed's big sheds close to the cattle pens. And on all three shifts there were the level-crossing-gates to be opened and shut, so in all there was plenty to do.

Every week Mr Gotobed's men would come down with big churns of new milk and wait for a train to come in with two vans of calves. These had to be unloaded and then each calf was given a good drink of the milk. I used to notice that if a calf sucked well it got a good lot of the milk, but if it was awkward it got the milk thrown over it, so the poor beast did not get much to drink.

Every morning Mr Gotobed, his two sons and four or five of his men came to the station with horse boxes full of calves. These had to be loaded onto nearly all the passenger trains throughout the day – some for the Norwich line, some for the Hunstanton line and others for the Cambridge and London lines. Up to twenty or thirty of the animals would have to be put into sacks which then had the tops sewn up before they were put into basket barrows ready for loading into the guards' vans. I hasten to say that the calves' heads were outside the sacks, but I always thought this a cruel way of moving the beasts because they used to struggle frantically and nearly strangle themselves, and they had to lie in those bags for hours on end with their legs bent.

Sheep often had to be unloaded on the night shifts and I found dealing with fifteen to twenty wagon-loads of them, in the dark hut having our supper we suddenly looked at one another and then at one of the mail bags from which was coming a ticking sound. We both had the same thought in our minds – a time bomb.

I fetched the Station-master who said the bag must not be opened; the best thing to do was to put it in the mail van and then the driver must run it down the road about a hundred yards away from the station. So this was done. All was then quiet until about half past after midnight we heard voices outside the hut and, as we peered out, we presently saw someone just going into the waiting-room. The mail driver said we had better telephone police, but I said I'd take a shunting pole and a hand-lamp and have a look round first, if he kept watch.

It was dark inside the waiting-room so I didn't feel like going in, and I just walked by flashing my lamp and calling out 'Good night'. I went to the end of the platform then turned and began to walk back, knowing that this time I *must* go in; but just before I reached the door a young couple came out and asked how long it would be before the down Mail came in. It appeared that they had been to a dance in Watlington and had missed the last bus back to King's Lynn, so had decided to go home by train.

That eased our minds a bit, but there was still that ticking going on in the mail bag. As soon as the down Mail had come in and the rest of the bags had been loaded on to it, the driver drove very carefully back to Downham where he called up the Postmaster who sent for the police. The bag was duly opened and inside was found the cause of our scare – an alarm clock which a woman at Clenchwarton was sending to her daughter in Denver.

When I first went to Magdalen Road the big crossing-gate hut stood near to where the signal-box does now, and only a fence separated it from the main highway to Watlington and Magdalen.

I never knew who might call in, when I was on night duty, and on my own, quite a job at first until I got to know the trick of doing it.

As soon as the doors of cattle wagons were dropped the cattle used to run out on their own, but sheep did not – they simply went round in circles inside the wagon and refused to come out, and the more they were hustled the worse they got. So I soon learned that the thing to do was to place a hand-lamp in the pens, catch hold of a sheep and hold it so that the light fell on to it, and to keep saying baa, baa, and then all the rest of the sheep came out without any bother. As Magdalen Road was the station for villages for many miles around we had a lot of livestock to deal with – cattle and sheep for shows all over the country, as well as prize bulls, heifers and rams on their way to America and other foreign parts. King's Lynn cattle market is held on Tuesdays, so on that day of the week we always had several van-loads of stock to be loaded and unloaded.

The mail for the London, Norwich and Peterborough routes was brought every night, at a quarter to ten, from Downham by a private firm in a red van bearing the letters Royal Mail. There were three mail vans on the Mail train which left King's Lynn at 10.25 – one at the front for London, one half-way down the train for Peterborough and one at the rear for what we called 'shorts'– that is for letters going to Norwich and other places near by. Three or four passenger coaches were attached to the train and it was a pleasant sound to hear, for ten minutes before the train left Lynn, the elderly, bearded ticket collector keep up an incessant chant of 'Wisbech – March – Peterborough – Ely – Cambridge – London. Any more for the Mail?'

One of the fastest drivers of the Mail was Harry Hall; the moment he got the green light he was off. When I was on night duty the local policeman often used to come and have a chat with me, and we really enjoyed watching the Mail train leave Magdalen Road, just before two o'clock in the morning, if Harry was on her.

The instant his fireman shouted 'Right, mate', he was away, and before he had gone three hundred yards he was almost at top speed, while the sparks and flames which leapt from the firebox as Tank Futter, the fireman, hurled on the coal were like a firework display.

I remember that one Sunday afternoon the Royal train went through on its way from Wolferton to London; the engine was due to return to King's Lynn at 6.10 p.m. Harry Hall was the driver, with Tank as his fireman, and the earliest we expected him at Magdalen Road was eight o'clock.

All the passenger trains had gone through so I went up to the signal-box to have a chat with my mate Herbert, and at twenty minutes past seven Ely North signalled that the Royal engine had passed through and was somewhere near Littleport. At that moment Downham signalled the engine, so I left the box to put the gate across and the engine went past us at ten minutes to eight. It was a dark, drizzly night and as it flew past us with the firebox open and the red glare from it lighting up the sky, the engine looked like something being driven by the devil. To do the journey from London in that time Harry must have averaged more than 60 miles an hour, allowing for his having to slow down at big stations, and this, remember, was fifty years ago.

One night, when we had unloaded the mails into the big basket barrows, the Mail train driver and I stood talking when he suddenly said: 'I think I just saw someone down the platform near the London mails – I'll just have a look.'

By the side of the platform were some big bushes and shrubs and behind these, over the fence, lay grass fields leading over to Holme Common. As the driver walked towards the end of the platform I saw someone come out of the bushes and presently the Mail driver came back and told me that a chap wanted a ticket for London.

'All right, I said, if he comes to the office I'll get him one.

But the driver said that the man dare not show himself a[s he] was on the run from the army and the police were after [him, and] would I take the ticket down to where he was hiding in the bu[shes] so that he could stop there till the last minute.

I got the ticket, took it to him and he paid for it. Then, whe[n the] guards showed their green lights he made a dash for the [train,] got in and I slammed the door and he was gone.

About a quarter of an hour later two policemen came p[uffing] and panting into the crossing-gate hut, wiping their brow[s and] wanting to know if I'd seen a soldier get on to the Mail[. Well] I told them I had not – only six people had got on and I des[cribed] them all, including the deserter who, though he was w[earing] khaki breeches, had a civilian jacket and jersey over them[and a] civilian cap on his head.

'That's him,' said the policemen, and they told me t[hat the] chap had jumped out of his bedroom window while the[y were] questioning his father, and had got away across the c[ountry] where he knew every inch of the land. They teleph[oned to] Liverpool Street, but I found out later that the deserter [jumped] off at Bishop's Stortford and it was some months before [he was] caught.

Another night we had a proper scare; it was at the ti[me when] the Irish Sinn Feiners had just blown up or set fire to so[me signal] boxes near London.

When the up Mail train came in a tall, smartly dresse[d man got] out and asked me if I had seen anyone loitering abou[t or any-]thing unusual. I told him I had not, so he said:

'Well, keep on the alert because the police have ha[d word] that there might be trouble tonight.'

Now there were always two mail bags which came [on the up] Mail for Downham from King's Lynn. These we wo[uld put in] the gate hut until the down Mail train came back, a[nd then they] would be loaded together. As the mail van driver and [I were] to have a chat or to ask for a night's shelter. I used to get poachers, drovers and tramps, and one night an old chap who offered up a loud prayer every hour.

On one occasion an old woman who used to go to King's Lynn three times a week to fetch a supply of laudunum, came off the Mail and, as it was pouring with rain, asked me if she could shelter in the hut until it was over. I knew her quite well so I told her to go inside and make herself at home. Ten minutes later I went in and found her sitting by the fire in my chair fast asleep, so I ate my supper sitting on my locker then went out to unload some cattle. When I returned she was still fast asleep. I was in and out of the hut most of the night, pulling the gate-locks or the levers to work the top set of points, and still she did not move. At about a quarter past five she woke up, looked outside and called out 'What's the time?'

When I told her she exclaimed: 'Good gracious, I'll have to go and get my old man's breakfast ready,' and off she set on her three-mile walk home.

Often an old drover named Jimmy Ling used to spend the night with me when he was drifting a big flock of sheep from some Norfolk sheep fair. Jimmy was over 80, a happy, cheerful man who never wore socks but wrapped rags round his feet. He and his dog must have walked thousands of miles driving herds of bullocks or drifting sheep, and nearly every Tuesday the pair of them spent the whole day at the Lynn market. When he was a young man Jimmy had once shot a gamekeeper and had been transported to Botany Bay for ten or twelve years.

Then there was another chap – a poacher who, one Saturday night, asked if he could spend a few hours with me. I was always glad of company so I said he could.

On Sunday mornings I finished work at two o'clock, after the down Mail had gone, but on this occasion I stayed in the hut until it was broad daylight and then we both set out together for about half a mile towards Magdalen Bridge. Then the man stopped.

'I'm just going over to Lottie Collins's rabbit stack to see if I can get a couple,' he said, and went through the hedge with his lurcher dog while I mounted my bicycle and rode home.

That evening, as I and some of my mates were coming out of church, we were stopped by our two local policemen who said they wanted a word with me. Then they asked me what time I had finished work that morning and if I had seen anyone about on my way home or heard a gun fired twice.

I told them that I had had a mate with me all night in the hut, though at first I would not tell them who it was. When they said, however, that anything I told them would go no further I gave them the man's name, and they were quite relieved to hear it. Apparently a farmer on the other side of the fen, about two miles away, had got up early hoping to catch someone who had been after his rabbits. He had spotted two dark forms by the side of some bushes and had called out:

'Come on out, I know who you are,' whereupon one of the poachers had said:

'Let's shoot the old b . . .' and two guns had gone off. The farmer had told the police that he was sure that one of the men was the one who had been with me all night in the hut, but after I had told the police about him they knew he could not possibly have been.

On yet another occasion, I remember, I was reading in the gate hut with both doors open. It was a hot, sultry night after a day when not a breath of wind had stirred. Then a storm broke. The rain fell in torrents for a good half-hour and when it stopped I must have dozed off because when I looked round the doors were still open. Then I heard something which sounded as if someone were running round the hut. I sat quite still but the soft, thudding noise continued, so at last I plucked up courage and went outside. No one seemed to be about and I went in again and soon found out where the sound was coming from. Half of the floor of the hut was bricked, the other half boarded. After the heavy rain a large toad had evidently found its way into the hut and it was the noise he made on the boards which I had heard. So there was nothing to be alarmed about, but at half past two in the morning, with no one about and everywhere pitch dark and very still, things seem very different from how they appear in broad daylight.

Some amusing things could happen on the station, though, in broad daylight. I remember that, on one occasion, a local train came in and before it drew to a standstill a vicar from a near-by parish stepped from his compartment, his back to the engine, and went spinning round on the platform several times before he finally landed backwards into Mr Paige's glasshouse. Fortunately, though, he was unhurt.

On another morning I was pulling a two-wheeled barrow loaded with a churn of milk, a box of eels and a big travelling trunk which belonged to a Mr Petchell who was returning to Canada. The platform, at that time, was not covered with tarmac but with sand and gravel, and it was the custom to run one of the barrow wheels on the stone slabs which bordered the line edge of the platform, and the other on the gravel. I had a bundle of letters in one hand and, as the train came in, I put a spurt on and the barrow keeled over, sending the trunk flying on to the metals in front of the approaching train. The driver put his brakes on hard but not in time to prevent the engine smashing the trunk and scattering its contents all over the track.

Mr Petchell was due to travel by a later train, so I was sent to his house with a letter instructing him to buy a new trunk in King's Lynn and to charge it to the railway; his belongings would then be repacked and sent by the afternoon train. When I got to the house Mr Petchell's mother came to the door. She took the letter, read it and remarked:

'Whatever did that fool of a porter think he was doing?'

'I don't know, mam,' I replied meekly, 'I wasn't there.' But Mr Petchell got a new trunk and I helped him to pack it and, in the end, everything went off all right, except for me getting a good telling-off for being so clumsy.

More Memories of Magdalen Road

The villages for four or five miles around Magdalen Road station were surrounded by woods, so during the 1914–18 war thousands of tons of timber were cut and carted to the station to be used for making pit-props and other things. The Canadian Forestry Corps was billeted on West-Winch Common, three miles away, and every day, month in and month out, steam traction engines would be hauling huge drays piled with timber to be loaded. About once a month, when everywhere was stacked high with wood, two cranes would arrive. These were wound up by hand, two of them lifting one enormous tree, and while they were working there was always plenty for us to do at the station, for there would be four or five timber bolsters ready each day to be attached to the goods trains which took them to the sawmills.

Among goods bought by the government for army use were baled hay and straw, so there were always stacks of these to be put on the land beside the refuge siding where they were guarded all the time by soldiers in case of fire or theft.

Milk was brought to the station twice a day, at half past nine in the morning and at half past five in the afternoon, in horse-drawn floats. The horses would be tied to the station fence and the churns loaded on to barrows and wheeled to the platforms to the spot where we estimated the milk van would stop. So much milk arrived that the Station-master asked, on one occasion, for an extra four-wheeled barrow which was delivered one Saturday morning. Six full churns were placed on it and then it was wheeled alongside the other barrows to be ready for the train. But for some reason the train went too far along the platform so we had to move all the barrows along, which is when the fun started.

An old man who was not very bright in the head used to drive a float from one of the farms, and on this morning he helped me with one of the barrows, but he was so scared that we should not get the milk on the train in time with our having to move the churns, that he pushed the load first into the side of the train and then on to a soft patch of sand on the platform which, as I have said earlier, was not then covered with tarmac. One wheel went down into the ground and over went a churn of milk. The Station-master and both guards flapped round us like hens, and people having breakfast in the restaurant cars looked through the windows laughing their heads off. I remember wishing that the platform would open up and swallow us all, I felt so confused.

Most of the farmers' horses which brought the milk knew just where to stop and once a rug had been thrown over them they settled down and took no notice of the trains blowing off steam. One pony, though, was not to be trusted. A land girl had driven it for about a week from Mr Jones's farm at Setch, when it bolted, overturned the float and threw off the girl, breaking her arm. Next day a soldier who was working on the farm was sent down with the pony, but again it ran away, breaking a shaft of the float and injuring the soldier.

About a week later I saw the pony again, driven this time by a lad about 17 years old. Thinking I was offering him some good advice I went over to him and told him to be sure to secure the animal safely to the fence. But he just threw the reins over the pony's back and said:

'He won't run away, he's only too glad to stand still,' and then I saw that lather and sweat were running off the animal's back and that it was puffing away like a steam engine. The boy told me that as soon as they'd started the pony showed signs of wanting to bolt.

'I didn't stop him,' he said, 'but gave him a few strokes on the ribs with this ash stick, and a few more when he tried to ease up.' That seemed to cure him, for he never gave any more trouble after that.

We did not always have such a pleasant-smelling thing as milk to load, however. Mr Birch of Watlington Hall kept a large pack of fox hounds and about twice a year a cart from there would make several journeys to the station loaded with three-hundredweight casks full of dog dung which we had to load into trucks to be sent to the Tanneries. Each cask had a strong door which was securely bolted and locked, which was a good thing for us because the smell was not exactly that of the finest French perfume.

For years before I started work on the railway it was the custom for the plate-layers to mow the grass on the sides of the lines every June and, a few days later, to pile it all into heaps. Then a ballast train would leave March or King's Lynn with a gang of men and the hay would be loaded into trucks and taken to a chaff factory at Littleport. This was always done early in the morning so as not to interfere with normal traffic. The train would keep moving slowly along while two men on each truck loaded and four men pitched to them from the line-sides.

One day in 1919 a strong gale was blowing, sweeping straight across the branch line to Wisbech and hourly getting worse. A goods train had left Middle Drove to call at Wiggenhall Siding which stands on the single line between the Ouse Bridge and the Middle Level Bridge, the line here rising steeply and having a sharp curve. The goods were bound for Magdalen Road and because the line was a single one the driver carried the Tablet to signify that no other train could occupy the line until the Tablet was given up. I might explain, perhaps, that the Tablet is a flat iron ring, about four inches across, which is carried in a pouch attached to a leather-covered hoop through which the driver or his fireman puts his arm when receiving the Tablet from a signalman. In some stations there are Tablet Catchers which have an iron arm on to which the driver can slip the Tablet if the signalman is unable to get down from his box to receive it himself. The signalman removes the Tablet from its pouch and places it in an instrument, two feet high, and then rings through on a plunger to the signalman at the next box who will at once reply. Neither man can then accept or issue another Tablet from the instrument until the line is clear. This method of signalling is used only on single lines to prevent two trains from being on one section at the same time.

Well, to return to this particular, windy day. The express from Hunstanton to Peterborough North had come in and still there was no sign of the goods train. The Station-master telephoned to Wiggenhall but could get no answer, so I climbed up the tallest signal post from which I could see the goods train half-way up the hill. Over half an hour later it finally arrived at the station and we learned that, on the sharp gradient before Wiggenhall Siding, the gale had blown the piled hay from the sides of the lines all across the track, making it impossible for the wheels to grip the rails. The fireman, the guard and the porter from the siding had had to clear all the hay away before the train could get over the bridge. This delayed the express and so this year was the last in which hay was carted by ballast train; since then it has always been burned.

As Magdalen Road was the best station for trains to Liverpool Street or to places reached *via* March and Peterborough, we used to get all the gentry from a number of villages, besides scores of big farmers. I got to know many of them and they would often chat with me if the trains were a little late.

One man I remember well was Mr Whitbread of the famous brewing firm. He used to drive in from Setch in a pony and cart and always wore a high, hard hat rather like an old-time Quaker's, and, even in summer, two or three overcoats. He came regularly once a week to 'see if there was anything for him', by which he meant was there any whisky. If some had been delivered he gave us a sixpenny tip, but only threepence if none had come. The whisky was in stone gallon jars with wicker round them, and he used to tear off the old labels and tie on fresh ones addressed to the friends to whom he was sending the jars.

Just before Christmas he used to drive up in the morning, tie his pony to the railings, put two thick rugs over it and then, telling me to keep an eye on it, would give me half a crown as a Christmas Box. Mr Paige, the Station-master, would then come hurrying out to meet him and the two of them would go round to Mr Paige's house, Mr Whitbread carrying a full bottle of whisky. Half an hour later they would come out, laughing and chatting, and then, after shaking hands with us all, Mr Whitbread would wish us a Happy Christmas and drive off back to Setch. Sometimes he used to call in to say that his housekeeper would be at the station next day and would I look after the tricycle, slipping sixpence into my hand as he asked. The housekeeper was a smartly-dressed, middle-aged woman who kept some lovely Dalmatian dogs. She always gave me a shilling for storing her tricycle and getting it out for her when she returned.

Christmas was a happy, busy time at the station in those days.

Trains might be a little late but no one seemed to mind. Children would be returning from boarding school and Christmas boxes for Mr Paige would arrive by the dozen – ducks, chickens, hares, rabbits, pheasants and even a turkey or two. Although some of the engines which pulled the trains were only the small ones we called Intermediates, the drivers did their best to keep on time despite the extra numbers of people travelling. I have seen those little engines, their fronts red hot, drawing more than a dozen coaches and yet coming in dead on time.

As we were such a busy country station there was a good chance of us getting tips not just at Christmas but all the year round. Most of the passengers were generous, but I remember the first time I met the Vicar from Holme. He came off the London train with a big case which I carried for him. He gave me a coin which I thought was a florin piece and which I slipped into my pocket, but when he had gone I looked through the loose money in my pocket and found only pennies, halfpennies and a sixpence. I mentioned this to my mate and he roared with laughter:

'That was a penny he gave you,' he said, 'you'll never get more than that from him.' When the reverend gentleman came to the station the next time I took particular note of what he gave me for carrying his case, and sure enough it was only a penny.

Another regular passenger I remember well was a Mr Box from Shouldham who came to Magdalen Road twice a week to fetch fish which arrived from King's Lynn and which he used to hawk round the villages. I used to help him to load the boxes on to his pony-driven trap and he always gave me something – a pint of shrimps or a mackerel, a pair of bloaters or, occasionally, a crab.

Another gift I often received was from one of the men who brought the milk from a near-by farm to be loaded on to the trains. Because he had a large herd of cows he would often bring me a bottle of beaslings – the rich thick milk given by a cow after calving, which makes very good custard.

In later years I could always count on being supplied with eating potatoes, early seed potatoes, and manure for my garden by railway customers, and on corn for my fowls and even a bale of clover hay for my pet donkey. On two occasions one farmer brought me an eight-week-old pig and he always told me that it was my own fault if I had no potatoes, chicken corn and so on, for I had only to tell him and he would let me have anything I wanted.

I think one of the strangest gifts I received was from a man whom I had been helping to unload potatoes. When we had finished he suddenly turned to me and asked if I liked blackbird pie. I told him I did, so next day, when he came along with another load of potatoes, he brought me six birds tied together by their necks, and handed them to me saying:

'There you are, Arty, they'll make you a good feed.'

Sometimes a goods train would have to shunt into the long refuge siding and stay there, either because the station ahead already had two or three trains shunting or because an express was due. There was one King's Lynn goods train which I never minded being shunted because Len Andrews, the fireman, used to call over to me:

'Arty, come and have some mussels.' He lived down among the Lynn fishermen and he always brought some live mussels with him which he would place on the coal shovel and hold for a time in the red-hot firebox so that, as he used to say, they cooked in their own juice. I must say I have never tasted better ones. Len was a very good pal of mine and I was very sad when he and his wife were killed in the Second World War by a bomb which fell on the Spread Eagle at King's Lynn.

When I was on night shift I used to go to bed after breakfast and get up about three o'clock in the afternoon. On Tuesday, May

10th, 1920, I took my gun, after I had had my tea, and went after some rabbits in Bushy Field. I was nicely hidden in some bushes when I heard someone calling me, but as I had really no business to be where I was I did not answer. As I peered through the leaves, however, I saw that it was one of my workmates so I went out to meet him. He told me that he had been round to my house where my mother had told him where he might find me; he had got her to pack some food for me as I was wanted on duty right away. As we walked along to the station he told me that poor old George Woodhouse, the crossing-gate keeper, had been knocked down by the Hunstanton to Liverpool Street train and was in a very bad way. I was to go and take charge of the gate.

Just as I reached the gate hut a lady came out and asked me to go for the doctor and let him know that Mr Woodhouse had just died. Poor old George, he had managed to save both the gates, except for a few iron rods which were broken when the engine hurled him against them, though he had been killed in doing so. I stayed on the gates from seven o'clock that Tuesday evening until Thursday afternoon when I was replaced by a relief gateman from Cambridge so that I could get home for a rest before going back on my normal shift at ten o'clock.

Although George Woodhouse had saved the gates, the following Sunday night they were smashed to pieces by the 10.52 p.m. Mail train from King's Lynn because the relief man had left them across the line. He was taken off the job, severely reprimanded – or made to walk the carpet as we used to put it – and was then sent to learn signals. Thirty years later I met him again; he was then a first-class relief signalman and finally became Inspector on March station.

In 1919 and 1920 the main topic of conversation round Magdalen Road and in the neighbouring villages was the oil which had been discovered at Setch, three miles from the station. A tall chimney was erected, with buildings alongside it, retorts were built and big offices, and a railway line was laid down with sidings and a signal-box. The box was called Clark's Drove and it stood roughly midway between Magdalen Road and King's Lynn. Hundreds of navvies came down and a host of clerks and chemists, while many farm workers left the land in order to earn big money in the English Oilfields as they were called.

All this made Magdalen Road an even busier station because most of the machinery and building material was unloaded there by crane to go on to Setch by road. There was even talk of a pipe-line being laid from the oilfields to King's Lynn. About once a week a number of high officials came from London in a special carriage attached to the 11.50 a.m. train; this carriage was uncoupled and taken to Clark's Drove by a special engine from King's Lynn which would be waiting in the down refuge siding.

I had a friend who worked on one of the oilfield retorts and he would often look in for a chat when I was on night duty. Several times I asked him if the oilfields were really going to be a success and he would reply:

'I'm afraid not.' As all the reports said that a large percentage of oil was being found in a medium quantity of shale I could not understand this until, one night, my friend explained it to me. He said that it was really quite simple; if crude oil was poured on to any ground which was then analysed half an hour later, a high proportion of crude oil would be found in each cubic yard.

A few evenings later the down train from London was several minutes late in arriving and waiting for it was Major Luddington, a big local landowner. Presently he came over to me and started talking of this and that and then he asked me what I thought of the English Oilfields. I told him I had not much faith in them, to which he replied that I must have a reason for saying that because the newspapers were full of the wonderful discovery that had been made and of how it would help to put England on her feet again after the war. So I told him what I had learned from my friend. This, said Major Luddington, bore out what his broker had told him when he had advised him to have nothing to do with the oilfields.

Incidentally, they did eventually prove a complete failure. The tall chimney remained as a memorial to them until it was blown down about three years ago, and at the same time the sidings and the signal-box were done away with.

It was in 1920 that an amusing incident occurred one Tuesday afternoon. Two well-known characters, Dobson Robertson and Loggins Wiffen, were travelling back from King's Lynn where they had spent the day at the cattle market and had, as usual, had a good few drinks. The train they caught was the 4.32 p.m. to Magdalen Road, made up, as most of the slow passenger trains were, of composite coaches, that is, coaches without corridors.

Just as the train was about to leave a woman, laden with shopping bags, entered the compartment. As soon as the train began to move Dobson looked up and said:

'I don't believe that if you pull that little chain it *will* stop the train, but I'll soon find out.' He stood up and stretched his arm towards the chain.

'You fool,' said the woman, 'of course it will stop it,' and she pulled him back on to the seat.

Then Loggins got up and began to open the carriage door, saying:

'If that fool pulls the chain then I'm getting out.'

'Look out,' screamed the woman, 'you'll get killed,' and she hauled *him* back to his seat, thus releasing her hold on Dobson who once again stood up and declared:

'I'm sure it won't stop the train.' Again the woman had to hold him down. This went on for ten minutes until they got to Magdalen Road; first one man saying he was going to stop the train, then the other saying he wasn't going to get summoned for what his pal did and threatening to jump out, and the woman trying to hang on to both of them at once.

As soon as the train drew in to Magdalen Road she got out and rushed up to the Station-master exclaiming:

'Thank God we've got here at last; I've been travelling with a couple of madmen.' But as soon as Mr Paige saw who the madmen were he burst out laughing:

'That's all right, ma'am, they're both as harmless as lambs – neither of them would have pulled that chain or jumped out; they only did it to tease you.'

Everything seemed to be going smoothly for me until one day in September 1921 when I and thousands of others who had been on the railway for less than five years, received redundancy notices because by then most of the men were back from the Forces and so the railways were overstaffed.

On the day I got my notice Major Luddington came to the station with one of his friends, and Mr Paige told them that I should not be carrying their cases much longer. When he had learned the reason Major Luddington said:

'Well, we're going to London today and we'll have something to say about that.' And so they did, because during the afternoon a message came from London cancelling my notice. Four days later, however, another notice came with a letter telling me that, although I had been given a good report, I could not stay on when so many others had to leave. So I left on September 12th and I thought that was the end of my days as a railwayman, but very soon came another letter asking me if I would accept a vacancy at Magdalen Road should one occur. I replied that I would. But it was April 2nd, 1923, before I heard anything more.

That day I was offered a job at Coldham as goods porter for three months until a platform porter's job fell vacant. I accepted and went to Coldham on April 9th; the three months became forty-two years and a day because I did not leave until I became redundant, for the second time, on April 10th, 1965.

At Coldham

My first impression of Coldham, I must confess, was not a very good one. I had been used to a much bigger and busier station where the platform porters kept themselves very smart, with well-polished buttons and shoes. When I first saw Coldham I nearly gave up the job on the first day. The signalman had a scarf round his neck and a cap turned half-way round, milking fashion. I don't think his boots had seen any blacking for months. A porter who met the train had a cigarette in his mouth – a thing which had never been allowed at Magdalen Road – and when he turned round I saw that he had a big hole in the seat of his trousers.

But I had not been many days on the station when I found that my impressions had been entirely wrong. The signalman turned out to be an exceedingly good friend, while Mr Jordan, the Station-master, could not have treated me better if I had been his son. He later became Master at the royal station of Wolferton where he stayed until he retired; he lives now at Wootton and we still correspond quite often.

Coldham at that time was only a small hamlet. Nearly all the cottages belonged to the Co-operative Wholesale Society which formed nearly three-quarters of the surrounding land. On railway time-tables the station was entered as *Coldham (for Peartree Hill)* and one of the Co-operative Society's farms is still called Peartree Farm.

The station was about four miles from March and three and a half from Wisbech, so all the fruit from as far away as St Germans Siding, Magdalen Road, Middle Drove, Sneeth Road, Emneth, Wisbech and Upwell Tram stations had to pass through Coldham on its way to the Midlands, the North and Scotland. Coldham itself dealt with large quantities, for during the season the Co-operative Society would load up to twenty vans of strawberries, each containing a thousand chips of the fruit, while other growers would load another ten between them daily. The firm of Messrs English Brothers, of Wisbech was the first to import aspen logs from the Baltic ports and use them for the manufacture of 'chip' baskets for the rapidly-increasing fruit trade. Most of the soft fruit which is now carried by road travels in cardboard containers.

My first job, as soon as I had alighted from the train that April 9th, 1923, was to load a truck with trussed hay, something I had never done before. But the man who had brought it to the station told me to pitch it to him and he would load for me. As soon as the truck was roped and sheeted with tarpaulin I had to load two trucks of grain and four of potatoes and sheet them. I began to think this new job was going to be heavy going but before long I thought nothing of having twenty or thirty trucks a day to load in addition to meeting passenger trains, looking after the lamps and sundry other odd jobs.

It was after I had climbed into the truck on that first day to help a man unload some potatoes that he asked me where I came from. When I said I was a Magdalen Man he asked my name.

'You're not Teddy Randell's son?' he asked.

'Yes,' I said.

He was so excited I thought he was going to kiss me. He told me that his name was Bob Wing and that he was working as horseman for the Co-operative Society and lived in a cottage near Coldham Hall. He had apparently lived at Magdalen when I was a baby and could remember me learning to walk when I was taken harvesting with my parents. He asked me where I was going to lodge, so I told him that I only wanted lodgings for alternate weeks as when I was on late shifts I could get home either by goods train or on my bicycle.

'There's a bed waiting for you at mine whenever you want one,' he told me; so for two years I lodged at his cottage and was treated like one of the family. Mrs Wing was a wonderful woman, always hoping they were making me comfortable and never letting me go out to work on the early shift at half past six unless she had cooked me a hot breakfast.

Although Coldham is only fourteen miles from Magdalen as the crow flies, and although both are in the Fens, I found that the dialect spoken by my new mates was quite different from mine. I used to wonder at first what they were laughing at when I shouted out to one of them; my Norfolk brogue seemed to amuse them. I even noticed differences in the hours that Coldham people worked. At Magdalen the men on the farms used to have a snack at nine o'clock in the morning, dinner from midday to one o'clock and then leave off at five o'clock, whereas at Coldham they worked on till eleven o'clock, had only half an hour for dinner and finished at four o'clock in the afternoon.

At Magdalen Road I had always been a platform porter and had never done any truck labelling, but at Coldham I had to do a lot of the latter and at times I found it a bit of a problem. All the Co-operative Society's potatoes, for example, went to Welsh stations which had names I had never heard of. Mr Jordan the Station-master or George Lusher the goods clerk always got the invoices ready and I would copy the routes from them, but one night the two of them went off early leaving the invoices ready to be put behind each truck label. They had apparently done the work in rather a hurry because one of the invoices I just could not read at all, though I could just make out that it was for Grays in Essex. I took the paper over to the signalman to find out what route these particular goods should take, but he could not read it either, so I did my best to copy it on the label just as it was written on the invoice. Then I labelled all the rest of the trucks and waited for the goods train to come in, hoping all the time that the guard would accept the truck I was not sure about. The train arrived, and I went round checking with the guards and when he got to the truck labelled Grays he just glanced at it and said:

'Grays – via London and Tilbury.'

Next morning I told the Station-master what a job I had had and he merely laughed:

'Grays goes on the L M S and then London – Tilbury – Southend via Stratford and Barking' so that was one route I never forgot after that.

Although there was always plenty of loading to be done at Coldham – potatoes, beans, corn, hay, mangolds and, after sheep-shearing, huge bales of wool – it was in June when the fruit season began that we were most busy. The Co-operative Society used to get about two hundred pickers down from London and employ another hundred or so local people and tramps. I have known six special trains packed with London pickers arriving to be met by horse-drawn vans and lorries which took the families to their living quarters in the neighbourhood. For the next few weeks Wisbech would be a lively place because the pickers went there to do their shopping and to drink in the pubs, and they needed quite a bit of keeping in order. I remember one day, when I was travelling home to Magdalen in the guard's van of the 5.32 p.m. passenger train from March, that a Detective Sergeant got in and joined us at Wisbech. The guard asked him what sort of a day he had had.

'I've never had such a b . . . day in all me life', said the Sergeant, who was a London man. 'Those pickers were everywhere and when I asked one to move out of the way he turned on me and asked me what the hell I thought I was. When I told him I was a police officer he asked me why the hell I didn't dress like one.'

The next night the Sergeant got in again with us and the guard asked him again how he had been getting on.

'Fine,' was the answer, 'no bother at all. I put my uniform on this morning and though some of the chaps kept looking me up and down I didn't get a mite of trouble out of them. It's the uniform they're scared of, you see, not the chap who's wearing it.'

There was always a policeman on duty on the Upwell to Wisbech steam tram line during the fruit season, to regulate traffic and to keep law and order among the pickers. This tram line, which is now closed although the track remains, began at Wisbech East station and ran across and alongside the main Downham to Wisbech road, over fields and over the canal then back to the road again, calling at Elm Bridge, Boyses Bridge, Outwell and Upwell. It carried both goods and passenger coaches. The carriages were very like those we see on old Western films, while all the engines had cow-catchers fixed over the wheels. Years ago those little engines made as many as eight trips a day, bringing thousands of tons of potatoes, sugar beet, corn and other produce in a single year besides conveying coal, fertilizers and seed potatoes to the various stations on the route. It was wonderful what those small engines could do. I have known them bring thirty-five to forty vans of fruit as far as New Common Bridge, about half a mile from Wisbech and then, because the bridge had a steep gradient and a sharp curve, have to leave half of the vans, go on to Wisbech and return to pick them up. When Wisbech Mart or Statute Fair was held the passenger coaches were packed with people, some of whom had to stand on the steps, but the buses killed the passenger trade and two years ago the Upwell line became redundant.

When I was still living in Magdalen, before my marriage, and travelling to and from Coldham on the weeks I was on day shift, I got to know several of the people who regularly used the Lynn to March train, and we got in the habit of riding together. Spuddy Whitrick, my mate, Ernie Humphreys who drove a petrol wagon, Sid Sly a painter and Ted Wilkin who was a carpenter working on some new houses which were being built in March. On Fridays we were joined by a King's Lynn fisherman who spent the first part of each week at sea and Fridays and Saturdays travelling to Peterborough and Whittlesey to hawk his fish round the villages. He always wore a round woollen hat, which we in Magdalen used to call a chummy hat, a thick navy blue woollen jersey, and leather boots reaching to his knees. Sometimes he brought his small, old-fashioned accordion with him and played and sang to us. His favourite song was *From the Dogger* (which he always pronounced Dorger) *Bank to Great Grimsby* which, so far as I can remember, began like this:

We sailed out in the sunset,
The Skipper and us three,
We set our course for the Dorger Bank
As we left our fam'lies in Great Grimsby.
Chorus
The wind it howled and the old man growled,
Ho, ho for a life at sea.

At the time I was at Coldham there were grass fields on each side of the chase which led up to the Hall where the Co-operative Estate Manager lived, and in them were hundreds of rabbits. The fields were, therefore, leased for shooting. Nearly every night, when I was lodging with Mr and Mrs Wing at their cottage near the Hall, I used to walk the mile and a half from the station, but on one occasion, as I wanted to go to a dance in Magdalen, I changed my duty hours and, as it turned out, it was a fortunate thing I did.

It was a lovely moonlit night and two men had gone with their guns into the fields where they hid themselves in the hollows. Then one of them came out and started walking and as only his head was visible to his companion the latter mistook him for a rabbit, fired and shot him through the head. Mr Wing was sent for and he and a fireman from Coldham station carried the dead man away in a horse rug. Had I been going back to my lodgings at my usual time I would have been passing just when the accident occurred.

My stay at Coldham was not to be very long for in 1925 I was offered the job of porter-signalman at Waldersea Siding and was given an eight-day instruction course in signalling. I passed my signal examinations and began my new work, taking charge of the signal-box, the crossing-gates and the siding. But I did not sever all connections with Coldham because Waldersea Drove Siding is only a mile from it, so Mr Jordan remained my Station-master.

Waldersea Siding

No lorries were used for transport when I went to Waldersea so all the potatoes, hay, straw, sugar beet and all the fruit from Friday Bridge and other districts around Wisbech were loaded at Waldersea to be sent off by rail. There were also two big farms – Lilypool and Jew House – near the Siding which were owned by the Co-operative Society and some of the finest horses in the country used to pull the wagons down to us, three horses to a a wagon; some of them did a three- or four-mile journey twice a day. There were other big farmers, too – A. H. Carter, A. G. Scott, George Flint and H. C. Flint – who seldom missed a day's loading between September and April or May, and they all had magnificent horses.

I remember one especially, an old rat-tailed called Jack which was owned by Mr George Flint. Jack was a regular visitor, coming down in a team of three daily, for nine or ten months of the year, and bringing huge loads of potatoes, corn or other produce. He was a wonderful animal, especially when, as often happened, we had trouble with van or truck doors which would not open because the load inside was pressed hard against them or, if they were of the sliding type, the runner on which they moved had become jammed. When this occurred, all we had to do was to hang the chains from Jack's fore-gears on to the door and he would pull, gently at first and then, if the door was badly jammed, harder and harder until at last he got it open. Never did he throw his weight at it or break anything, and I often thought what a marvellous horse he would have been on the railway for moving wagons.

All day the yard would be full of horses and wagons, and we had many exciting moments with them. Young horses, which were always driven in the middle of the team, sometimes threw themselves down, for example, and nearly chocked themselves on the chains. Sometimes an overhanging load on a two-wheeled cart would lift the horse off the ground so we had to cut it down, but the horsemen were prepared for anything and never seemed to get in a panic. Today not a single horse goes over the level crossing, yet only thirty years ago, on wet mornings, there would be gangs of them going over to the blacksmith's to be shod, a job which was nearly always done on rainy days.

Very often the horses and wagons would have to wait all day in the yard because we had no empty trucks in, and if none arrived they would have to take the potatoes or beet back to the farms and come down again on the following day. I always think this was the beginning of the end of railway transport for it happened week after week during the winter months and, in my opinion, was largely caused by slackness on the part of some officials.

Wisbech or Whitemoor supplied us daily with empty trucks. If we ordered thirty and they had plenty they would send us forty, with the result that we had to return ten as we had no room to store them. But if we ordered thirty and Wisbech or Whitemoor were short, then we often got none at all. And there was a constant demand at Waldersea for trucks. Seed potatoes arrived every day from Scotland and they had to be unloaded ready to be loaded up again the next day. Sugar beet, at that time, was not loaded under permit issued by the factory; growers would simply order what trucks they wanted and bring the beet down to us. If the factory was getting too many trucks in then we would be given the order to stop all loading until further notice. This very often meant that when trucks *did* arrive, farmers who had been waiting for them could not use them because the factory had told us to send them no more loads. Sometimes I used to take a risk and let the farmers load the trucks so that, when we got the all clear from the factory, I could have a train-load of beet ready to go at once. But it was a risk, and if any high officials had been about I should have been made to walk the carpet.

When I had been at Coldham I had thought that we were very busy during the fruit season, but I soon found that the work there had been nothing to what it now was at Waldersea. At Coldham fruit had come in regularly, day by day, enough to fill up a truck each time, but at Waldersea there were over a hundred growers and we could not really start loading until half past one in the afternoon; between half past two and four o'clock the place was a bedlam. Our empty vans and the empty trays returned from the fruit merchants would come up on the overnight goods train from Wisbech so that the first job each morning was to go round the trucks and book everything in. After that the vans had to be swept out and labelled with the names of the stations to which the fruit was being sent – Blast Lane, Sheffield, Leeds, Liverpool, Wigan and a host of others. When all this was done we were ready for the fruit to arrive from the farms.

Extra staff to help with loading were sent in the fruit season to all the stations in the Wisbech area while clerks came from London and elsewhere to assist with booking for three months. On Coldham station we had, besides the regular staff, two more full-time men while at one o'clock the three plate-layers, the three clerks and the Station-master would come along to help and at all the fruit stations there were representatives of the big fruit-buying firms, their job being to help to arrange the loadings and to check the quantities going into each van.

More than half of the soft fruit which we loaded went to the big jam makers, the rest was sent *on the market,* that is, to be sold by auction. Most of it was in trays, each holding 14 or 21 pounds, or in chips containing from 2 to 6 pounds each. When the first gooseberries arrived they were in 4-stone bags, being hard and green, but as soon as they began to ripen they came in trays or in 12-pound chips. Raspberries were loaded in chips or, if very ripe, in small tubs.

Waldersea Siding closed officially at four o'clock in the afternoon but often, long after that time, the yard would still be full of horses and wagons and there would be a long string of traffic waiting to get in. A special engine and guard's van used to arrive at 3.45 p.m. and not a moment would be wasted by the man in charge. The brake would be left on the main line and the engine put into the yard where the guard would go round coupling up all the vans, checking the labels and seeing that the doors were securely fastened. When the last load of fruit was on board, the engine would back over to the London trains then on to the trains going via Peterborough so that the joint line traffic was next to the guard's brake-van.

The train was due away at a quarter past four, but it was often still at Waldersea at half past and Wisbech would be ringing up to say that the south-bound fruit train was ready to come in. Everyone would be rushing madly about, and the clerks would ride on the train so that they could continue with their invoicing. The train stopped at Coldham to collect more fruit there and this is when trouble was likely to start. All during the afternoon engines would have been leaving March Locomotive Depot in twos and threes for Wisbech and Magdalen Road, all of them returning with fruit-filled trucks. When our train left us Wisbech telephoned the first fruit train going to Scotland; it would arrive at Waldersea and there have to stop because Coldham still had our train and was unable to shunt it because of engines and passenger traffic on the down line.

As soon as I could get the train out for Coldham and get rid of the Scotsman, Wisbech would ring the second Scottish train due to leave King's Lynn at 3.20. This, like the first, would have to stop. This is what railwaymen call 'being on the block', and for several years until the first fruit traffic began to go by road, fruit trains would be 'on the block' at Wisbech, Waldersea Siding, Coldham and Whitemoor Junction.

Although my day's work should have finished at eight o'clock in the evening I was never able to leave until nine o'clock and I have sometimes had to be on duty until after the Mail train had left Wisbech at seven minutes past eleven.

During the fruit season it was the custom to send a lad-porter of about sixteen or eighteen to Waldersea to learn the ways of goods-working and to help with the level-crossing gates. Most of them were very good lads but one, I remember, was outstanding. He was quick to learn, was polite and willing to help and was one of the best I have ever known in learning railway regulations or anything connected with signals. He spent four fruit seasons with me before he went to be resident gatekeeper at Sneeth Road, but he did not stay long because he went into Signals and before I left the railway in 1965 he was my Signals Inspector and is now the Divisional Signalling Inspector at March. In addition to all his railway activities he is a Justice of the Peace, the General Secretary of the Ely Labour Party and holder of several other important offices. His name is Henry Orbell and he never passes Waldersea without calling to see me. I can remember that when he was with me there was a very sharp signalman at Wisbech Goods Junction who knew all the rules and regulations by heart and he would sometimes ring me up to try to catch me out on some tricky question. Our old telephone had two ear-pieces, so as soon as he asked me something I could not answer I would say 'Just a minute, I can't hear you very well'. Then I would give Harry a wink and he would take the other ear-piece and when the signalman repeated the question would whisper the answer to me.

'Cor, the signalman would say, you *are* getting sharp at regulations.' I am not ashamed to say that if Harry had not been there I certainly would not have known all the answers.

After the rush of the soft fruit season was over the apples, pears, early potatoes, green onions, peas and broad beans would start to arrive. As well as all these there was hay or baled straw to be dealt with too. This had to be sent off in the morning because when there was fruit about there was no room in the yard in the afternoon for handling it.

During the Second World War fruit vans were very hard to get because the army was using so many of them. We had, therefore, to load strawberries in open wagons and once I had to put a ton and a half of trayed ones into a greasy coal truck; I have often wondered what condition they were in when they reached Sheffield.

Our three plate-layers, as I have said, used to help with the loading during the fruit season and they were experts at the job. When I first went to Waldersea, before I got the hang of things, they would often tell me to get on with the labelling during the rush hour while they attended to the strawberries.

Plate-layers' work was much harder then than it is now, for they had no hydraulic jacks and no gauges. Two men had to use heavy iron bars to lift the rails, while another hammered the slag under the sleepers with a tool known as a 'beater'. This is now done by a machine.

During re-laying operations all the rails and sleepers had to be unloaded by hand, the men heaving the rails from the ballast train by means of heavy iron bars and slewing them into position as they dropped them over the wagon side; this could be a very dangerous manœuvre. Then, when the re-laying was completed, the old rails and sleepers had to be removed again by hand; today machinery does all this. The new, flat-bottomed rails arrive on special, long trucks and are unloaded by small cranes controlled by the re-laying Inspector who gives the signal to the men to start winding. When each length of rail is clear of the truck it is pushed over and lowered on to big wooden blocks, and the ballast train then moves along and the same operation is repeated until all the rails are unloaded.

To load the old rails and sleepers is even more simple, for after they are unbolted the entire lengths are lifted bodily by a large steam crane and neatly stacked on to long, flat wagons.

Yet even without these modern devices, track could be re-laid quite quickly several years ago. In 1929, for example, the up line for Wisbech was re-laid for a distance of one and a half miles on two Sundays, on the second of which it poured all day with rain. All the old rails and sleepers were loaded up in one day, without a crane. It was a fine piece of work, and it has lasted too, for that piece of track is still in.

A very old friend of mine, Joe Day, was for many years a ganger at Waldersea Siding and one year he won a prize for the best-laid length of track in the district. He could get a stretch of rail as level as a billiard table, and all by eye for he had no spirit level. He used to kneel down and peer along the track and in this way was able to spot any defect which had to be put right.

The Decline of Waldersea

No one expected the fruit grown around Friday Bridge, Wisbech and Waldersea to go by any other means than by rail, but in about 1926 or 1927 a big lorry arrived one day and parked just outside our goods yard gate. Presently one of the fruit agents began to stop some of the lorries which were coming down the road bringing strawberries for us to load, and we saw the fruit being transferred to the parked lorry.

'That's a bit of cheek,' said Mr Jordan, the Station-master, while some of the porters remarked that the fruit would be in a fine state by the time it got to Sheffield market – it would be like so much pulp, after being jolted all that way on the road.

'Well,' said one of them as we watched the lorry drive away, 'I'm sure we shan't see *that* again.' But we did, for that lorry came every day, and from then on our loadings began to dwindle.

The next year brought two or three lorries and by 1930 we were only getting half the fruit we were used to handling. Then lorries which up to then had been used to bring sugar beet down to the goods yard began to take it themselves to the factories. The same thing happened in the case of potatoes, so that instead of loading twenty or thirty trucks a day we were only loading ten or twelve.

A good deal of this was the fault of the railway because there were very many occasions when we had no empty trucks or, if we had them, we were without sheets to cover them. Moreover, we were given strict instructions that we were not to have more trucks than were needed for one day's loading. This meant that if I had orders which I knew would fill twelve trucks, and I had the chance of getting twenty, I was not allowed to have them but had to let them go back to Whitemoor. I am afraid I did not always do this, but it meant falsifying the Stock Report, which I could do unless the Truck and Sheet Inspector came round and then I had some explaining to do.

I remember one morning I had telephoned my Stock Report to the Station-master and about half an hour later he rang through to tell me that some important official from King's Cross was on his way to ask me about the wagons I had in hand.

'And I hope your stock is the same as you gave me over the 'phone,' he said. He nearly fainted when I told him I had eight empty wagons extra.

The official duly arrived with his spats and umbrella and asked me if I would be loading up all the trucks I had in.

'No,' I said, 'I hope not, anyway.'

'What's that,' he replied; 'don't you know that you should only have enough for one day's loading?'

'Yes,' I said, 'I know that all right.'

'Then why on earth have you got those eight extra ones?' So then I explained how, nearly every day, I had to refuse farmers who had brought potatoes or other produce in horse-drawn wagons from over three miles away, and how very often they had to go back home and come down again the next day, and all this because, when I could have a few extra trucks, I wasn't allowed to.

'If *you* were a farmer,' I said, 'would *you* like it?'

'No,' he agreed, 'I must say I certainly wouldn't.' He listened carefully to all I told him then said he would make arrangements for me to have two days' supply of trucks. So for the next few weeks everything was all right, but then matters went back to what they had been before and no one seemed to bother.

Very often strings of empty wagons would pass through Waldersea but, as I had only one set of cross-over points, I could only detach trucks for the up road. One day I had twelve men waiting in the yard with loads and not a single truck to offer them. Just as I was thinking I should have to tell them to go back until next day, the telephone bell rang and on answering it I found it was an inquiry about a special train of sixty empty trucks due for Wisbech Harbour. So I took the opportunity to ask if I could have twelve if I could arrange to get them into the goods yard. I was told that I could, though I was not at all sure how on earth I *was* going to get them in the yard. Anyway, when the train arrived, I uncoupled twelve wagons, let the engine put them over on to the up road and then, when the train had gone, the twelve waiting men and I pushed those trucks, four at a time, into the yard.

One local agent, a Mr Overland who loaded fifty to a hundred tons of potatoes a day for Daniels of Bishopsgate said that he would hold himself responsible for any risks I ran if only I could keep him supplied with trucks. It was during a sharp spell of frost that he made this offer, and when I did get some trucks for him I had no sheets to go over the tops. When the potatoes arrived they were as hard as stones, but Mr Overland said it would be all right to load them while it was still frosty, but we would have to stop as soon as a thaw set in. On two days the only trucks I could get were cattle wagons, open all the way round, but still Mr Overland came down each morning from Outwell and said: 'No matter what you've got, keep us going with empty trucks of some sort and I'll keep *you* going with loads, for they're crying out for potatoes in London.'

So the work went on, and I must be one of very few railwaymen who for over five weeks of freezing weather, loaded bullet-hard potatoes into wagons with no straw or tarpaulin sheets to cover them.

Snow and frost not only made loading difficult but also faced the growers with the problem of how to get their produce down to the goods yard. Towards the end of the Second World War we had several periods of sharp frost and some heavy snowfalls of up to three or four feet deep. The snow was particularly thick on the mile-long stretch of road leading to the siding, so nearly all traffic stopped except for Mr A. H. Carter's Dumpers. These were a kind of tractor-truck in which the driver sat over the front wheels with no protection against the bitter weather, but as the wheels were very high they could move easily in deep snow. The Dumpers could only carry forty hundredweight each, so the two drivers, Jack and Monty Jeffries, had to do the journey three times a day, and no one ever saw them anything else but bright and cheerful. As Bob Band the blacksmith remarked: 'Those two bors deserve a medal for what they're doing in this weather.'

In the days when only horse-drawn wagons were used to bring goods to the siding, I have seen horses go down like ninepins as they tried to back their huge loads up to the goods trucks, all farm wagons having to be unloaded from the back.

One of our biggest suppliers, and so one for whom I always tried my best to get trucks, was Ted Harvey who had lived most of his life in Friday Bridge. In his early days he had been a real horseman, then he had sold most of his animals and gone in for motor lorries, eventually owning a fleet of six. He, his three sons and a son-in-law were all in the business and every day they brought great loads of potatoes, corn and sugar beet to the yard to be loaded up. During the Second World War we often had to make do with coal trucks which we called Bob Holes. These were very difficult to load because they had tall sides and a doorway which was only about two feet high. This meant that we had to put each bag of potatoes in, end first, and then climb into the truck to stack. This could be slow work, but the Harveys got through it quicker than most because they thought nothing of throwing seven and a half tons of potatoes over the truck sides. When Ted was nearly seventy he brought eight tons of potatoes down one day and, as I was helping him to load them, he picked up a hundredweight sack under each arm and carried them, unaided, over to the truck.

'I just wondered, Sonny,' he said, 'if I could still carry them like I used to fifty years ago.'

He was a tough, strong man but he had one weakness, and that was for the sheet string, as we called the four-foot lengths of tarred rope with which we tied the tarpaulin sheets down over the trucks. Every time that Ted came down to the station – and this might be three or four times a day – he never failed to ask me:

'Sonny, can you set me up with a few bits of sheet string?' When he got them home he used to hide them so his sons should not find them, but I think he often forgot himself where he had put them.

As time went by our traffic became smaller every year as more and more motor lorries took loads through to towns and factories instead of bringing them to us to send. Instead of having four or five men and a number of clerks to help me during the fruit season I was able to manage with the help of a lad, while later still I was completely on my own, working the signal-box and the crossing-gates and loading in the goods yard.

My busiest time was now from November to March with the Scotch seed potato traffic which still came by rail, and I had, besides, several trucks of potatoes a day to load for Smith's Crisps. Years before I used to think how nice it was at the end of

May when, with all the old potatoes gone, we had a lull until the second week in June when the first strawberries came along. We had a chance, then, to clean up everywhere in readiness for the coming season, but as time went by it became a welcome sight to see a load come in at all for we then got a chance of having someone to talk to.

There were other changes, too. Instead of the old steam engines coming in with the drivers we had known for years, we began to get diesels with strange drivers, for the really old hands never learned to drive these new arrivals on the scene. So that was the end of our taking out the coal scuttles to be filled, and how we missed those times when a nice big lump had rolled off the top of the tender. We were only allowed fifteen hundredweight of coal a year, but the big shut-up stove in the signal-box burned half a hundredweight a day, so you can imagine how we regretted the passing of the old steam engines.

But though traffic was so small and things so very quiet I did get a little bit of excitement one morning. I had just opened the crossing-gates when I saw two men coming down the road, both of them on a lady's bicycle. They asked me if passenger trains stopped there and I told them that, if they did, I had to give a good reason why. Then they inquired where they could get a train to Peterborough.

'You can get one at March,' I said, 'but where have you come from.'

'Wisbech,' replied one of the men after a bit of hesitation.

'Then why in the world didn't you catch one there?' I asked, but to that neither of the men replied and in a minute or two they rode away. I watched them, for I thought their behaviour a bit strange, and I had the feeling they were up to no good.

A tractor driver had left his bicycle near a stack close to the roadside and as I watched from my box, I saw the man who had been riding on the handle-bars of the lady's machine, jump down, run over and grab the bicycle from the road, mount it and ride off with his companion down the road. I telephoned the police in March and told them what I had seen and suggested they sent more than one sergeant to look into things as the men looked rough customers. In less than a quarter of an hour a police car with three officers and the two men inside came over the crossing and next morning a police officer came down to take a statement from me and to thank me on behalf of the Wisbech Superintendent, because those two men had stolen £750 worth of television sets and other goods. Later I received a cheque from the Insurance Company and a letter from the Chief Constable of the Isle of Ely.

Some time later I saw the men who were concerned in a wages snatch at March when over £20,000 of railway wages were stolen. I noticed them drive over my level crossing twice in ten minutes, just twenty minutes before the hold-up, though of course at the time I did not think much more than that it was strange a car should go backwards and forwards in so short a time. Later I picked out a photograph of one of the men in the car from a number of pictures shown me by Scotland Yard men, and I was asked to go to Brixton Gaol to an identification parade, but the man whom I had seen was not among the eighteen who were lined up in front of me.

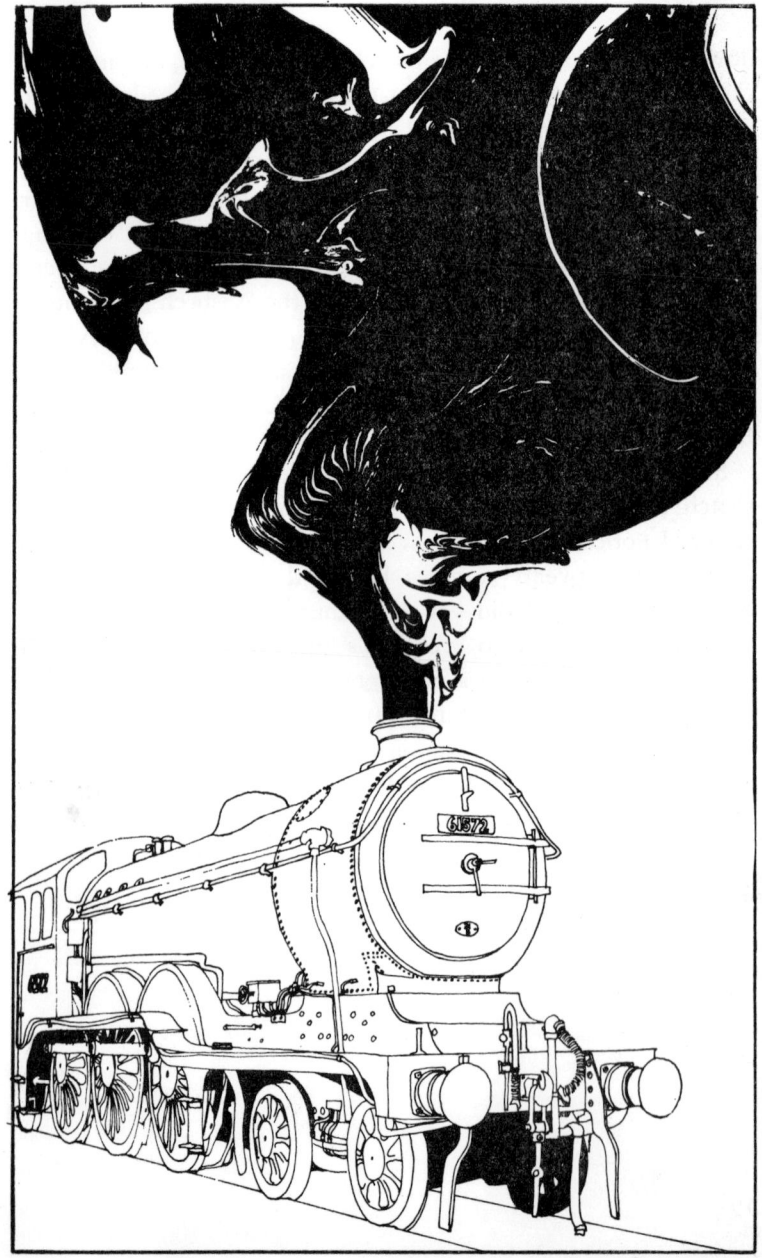

Whitemoor Marshalling Yards and Old Steam Engines

When the great railway strike of 1927 ended stocks of coal began to pile up faster than the railways could handle them. During that winter the up line between Coldham and Whitemoor Junction at March was closed for thirteen weeks and the whole line, with the exception of the level crossings, was packed with coal trucks which were added to, at both ends of the column, every weekend. On Saturdays, therefore, I had the job of walking along the track, pencil and pad of paper in hand, to take down the numbers and the destinations of the wagons. This list I handed to an Inspector from London or to the Inspector at March who had the responsibility of getting all the trucks moved so that the line could be filled up again. All this meant single-line working between March and Coldham, which was convenient for me as I could keep on the Fenman express instead of having to cycle to my lodgings from Wisbech, or could catch any train, expresses included, home to Magdalen Road.

Whitemoor Junction had always proved a bottle-neck for the coal trains which had to pass through it on their way to London and the Eastern Counties and which were frequently delayed there because of the limited space for shunting. Conditions in 1927, following the railway strike, became so chaotic that, in order to speed up shunting operations, it was decided that large marshalling yards should be built at Whitemoor. As I have already referred several times to these yards, which have done so much to improve traffic conditions, it will not perhaps be out of place to give a short account of them.

March, the nearest passenger station, is an important junction which has lines radiating to the west, to the Midlands *via* Peterborough, and to the north through Spalding, Lincoln, Doncaster, York and on to Scotland. The big problem, before the Up Yard was opened in March 1929, was, as I have said, how to receive and sort quickly the traffic from the areas north, east and west of Doncaster, from the collieries and yards of the Great Central section and from the Nottinghamshire and Derbyshire lines and send it on to London and East Anglia. The new Up Yard dealt with the huge amount of traffic quickly and efficiently, and so a Down Yard was planned so that work could be concentrated at one large centre which could deal quickly and at the lowest possible cost with a far greater number of wagons than the old yards had been able to handle. The Up Yard, for example, can hold 4,500 wagons compared with the 2,300 which could be got into the old yards on the west side of the main line north of March; these were eventually enlarged to take 6,600 so that the total capacity of the Up Yard is over 10,000 wagons.

This Up Yard consists of ten reception sidings and forty-one sorting sidings, while in addition there are four to hold 160 crippled wagons together with more sidings leading to cattle pens and to the Tranship Shed. This shed was built in sections in the woodyard of Messrs English Brothers at Wisbech Harbour and was taken to Whitemoor on a special train. The sections were so large that they overhung the track, so all down-line traffic had to be stopped while the train travelled with its great load, the

Inspector riding on the engine. Into the shed, which could hold up to twenty wagons, trucks were shunted so that small consignments of goods could be transferred from one truck to another; large wooden platforms built level with the floors of the wagons enabled goods to be wheeled easily from truck to truck.

Trains enter the Up Yard reception sidings at the north end and after the wagons have been examined and uncoupled into *Cuts* or sections bound for the same destination, the wagons are pushed over the Hump which is constructed with these gradients.

Arrival Roads   1 in 201   825 yards
Approach   1 in 77   42 yards
Ascent   1 in 50   27 yards
Crown of Hump
First descent   1 in 18   13 yards
Descent   1 in 130   45 yards
Final Level   200 yards

At the foot of the Hump are four hydraulic retarders of the Improved Frohlich type which were installed a few years ago by Metropolitan Vickers, each of them controlling wagons running into a group of ten sidings. The retarders are controlled by two men from a specially constructed tower, while a third man operates a switchboard which controls the electric motor working the several points leading to the sorting sidings. When a train is *Cut Up,* or divided into sections on the Hump, a shunter makes a *Cut Card* on which is indicated the number of wagons which have to be shunted into the various sidings. These cards are sent by pneumatic tube to the central tower where each operator receives a copy. The shunter controlling the point movement is able, by manipulating levers on the front of the switchboard, to store up in drums the route movements for the first seven pairs of points so that the wagons, when passing over these points, automatically set them for the following wagons. The signal which controls shunting movements is fixed at the crown of the Hump; it is a three-aspect, semaphor, upper-quadrant signal and indicates to the driver the speed needed to propel wagons over the Hump. In foggy weather a Klaxon horn is used, and there is a loudspeaker telephone communication between the Inspector at the top of the Hump and the shunters in the control tower. By this new method of shunting a train of seventy wagons, divided into forty or fifty *Cuts,* can be shunted in seven minutes, while the provision of rail brakes – Whitemoor Marshalling Yards were one of the first to have these – and of automatic points has meant that shunting has been speeded up tremendously compared with the old method of doing it by hand.

The Down Hump Yard is almost a replica of the Up Yard; it has reception sidings capable of taking 926 wagons, forty-one sorting sidings which can hold 3,567 wagons, and four more sidings to take 230 crippled wagons. In the Up Yard the electrical installations and mechanical brakes are of German manufacture, but in the Down Yards they have been made and installed by a British firm, while the retarder, known as the *Eddy Current Rail Brake,* a product of the Westinghouse Brake & Saxby Signal Company, is based on a different principle from the one in the Up Yard.

The brake is electrically operated and has an electro-magnetic action. When the wagon wheels enter the brake they are held by magnetic attraction, and when this is fully applied only twenty to thirty per cent of the braking force is due to friction. No matter how fast a wagon is travelling it always enters the brakes with perfect smoothness, and the higher the degree of energy applied to the brake the more the wagon is held down to the track.

In 1931 the old yards at Norwood, north of March, were remodelled and extended; they consist of two reception sidings which can hold 160 wagons, eleven marshalling sidings to take 930 wagons, and there are three Tranship Sheds capable of accommodating 200 wagons. In the evening and throughout the night fast goods trains arrive from London and East Anglia and, in a very short time, are shunted and sent off to Manchester, York and the Midlands. About 2,300 coal wagons are shunted daily at Whitemoor and sorted into train loads to go to Doncaster, Colwick, Lincoln, Mansfield and other places.

For the benefit of those interested in figures, here is a summary of the extent of the March marshalling yards which, when they are lit up at night, look like a small town.

The Up Yard, opened 1929
Number of Sidings   81
Total length in miles   31
Total area in acres   68

The Down Yard, opened 1931
Number of Sidings   67
Total length in miles   30
Total area in acres   50

Norwood Yard, extended 1931
Number of Sidings   23
Total length in miles   8
Total area in acres   14

Total area of Railway Property at Whitemoor   250 acres

Greatest number of Trains dealt with in 24 hours in each yard
1.8.1942,   Up Hump Yard,   69 trains,   2,841 wagons,   2,342
16.2.1943,   Down Hump Yard,   77 trains,   3,891 wagons,   1,685
3.9.1947,   Norwood Yard,   50 trains,   1,974 wagons

As I have never been a Loco man I do not profess to understand steam engines, but they have been so much a part of my life that I feel I must write a little about those that I have known. Diesel engines are, I know, fine and powerful and can run more cheaply but, along with many other people, I still miss the thrill of watching a steam engine pull out of a station or haul a heavy train up a hill. I miss, too, the sound of a train, two or three miles away perhaps, coming towards me on a still, frosty night, and the sight of the open firebox lighting up the sky with a bright glare and a shower of glittering sparks.

When I first started work on the railway the old engines of the Great Eastern were much smaller than those in use when I left; when we became the London North-Eastern Company we were given engines from the North-Eastern and Great Central areas – 'foreign engines' the old drivers called them.

Some of the old engines I first knew had been rebuilt at Stratford in the early 1900s and it was remarkable what punishment they could take; many of them had originally been built in Doncaster. To my mind some of the most outstanding were the small ones which the drivers called *Intermediates,* which pulled both passenger and freight trains. They worked the passenger trains with the Westinghouse brake and I have seen them hauling long lines of carriages and restaurant cars and still running to time. Their number ran, I believe, in the 62789 group. I also recall a freight and passenger engine which, built in 1883 or 1884, was still going strong in 1918.

Then there was the small tank engine such as was used on the Stoke Ferry line to pull mixed loads between Stoke Ferry and Downham. I once saw one of these pull seventy-three loaded trucks of sugar beet from Downham to Wessington Beet Factory. The siding at Downham could then hold only fifty trucks, so while the little pilot engine was taking on water, the tank engine squeezed the trucks of beet tightly on to the buffer stops where we pinned down about a dozen brakes. The trucks stood out of the siding on a curve leading to the Main line, and when the pilot backed on with plenty of steam we released the brakes and so gave the tank engine a bit of help in starting. As each truck moved she gained more speed, and when at last we saw that the guard's brake-van was moving the signalman telephoned to Denver telling the signalman there not to stop the train under any consideration or she would never get going again. Although she had to negotiate a very sharp curve where the branch line left the main line at Denver, the little engine kept the train moving and reached Wessington Beet Factory without a mishap.

Another passenger engine which was used on the old Great Eastern Railway, mainly on express trains, was in the No. 61312–61380 series, but I believe there was a smaller type also in use when I first went to Magdalen Road. All these engines I have mentioned were built for the Great Eastern Company and had the old crest on their sides. Later we had engines from the north of England, from anywhere in the London and North Eastern division and, during the Second World War, we even had engines which had been built in the United States.

I might mention, too, one Great Eastern Railway engine which, though it never worked in East Anglia so far as I remember, was considered the best of its time. It was the famous *Claud Hamilton,* which was put on show at the Paris Exhibition in 1900. Later, engines of the same type and class were used in East Anglia and one always worked the Royal Train from Wolferton to London. In 1918, and for several years afterwards, the Royal Train coaches were stabled at King's Lynn, but later, when the Royal family travelled by train, the coaches were brought to Wolferton and the royal sheds in King's Lynn were pulled down.

As Magdalen Road was on the main line from King's Lynn to Liverpool Street we saw quite a lot of the Royal Train. It passed through Waldersea two or three times a year, often with the Queen of Norway on board. When the train was booked to pass through, every station concerned received special workings, or notices, marked *Strictly Private,* one for each Station-master. These workings gave the *Special Rings* reserved for the train –

4-4-4; if the Royal family were travelling to Scotland then the mileage to each station and the times at which the train would stop to change engines were also given. No one was allowed in the goods yard adjoining any station on the line; gates were locked ten minutes before the train was due and all level crossings were manned by flagmen.

After the heavy bombing of some towns in the North-East during the Second World War, the King and Queen went from Sandringham to visit some of the most badly-hit areas and so passed through Waldersea where I was on duty as signalman. On the previous Sunday both gates at the level crossing had been run through by a train and one big gate-post had been knocked down; the only protection for road traffic, therefore, was a rope stretched across the road and guarded by a plate-layer with flags and detonators. According to strict rules and regulations I was not allowed to pull my Distant Signals off, so when the Royal train was approaching my signal-box my signals were at Caution, causing the driver to wonder what was the matter and to give a prolonged blow on his whistle. The Inspector who always travelled on the engine and the Inspectors who were on the train all had their heads out of the windows, for they thought something must have gone wrong. This happened on the Tuesday of that week, on both the outward and the return journey, and again twice on the Thursday; I am, therefore, one of the very few signalmen who have ever checked the Royal train four times in one week without it being shown in the special workings. It was always a wonderful sight to see the train go through, the coaches glittering in the sun and the big green engine polished and shining, with its buffers painted white. It is several years, though, since it has passed through Waldersea and this year, 1967, the royal station at Wolferton has been closed.

One small type of goods engine worked most of the branch line freight trains in East Anglia. I remember once that a King's Lynn driver, Peter Jackson, was returning to Lynn with fifty trucks of coal and slag and had been passed by Whitemoor to come close in front of an express. Jackson, one of the best drivers on the run, wanted to get home early as it was Saturday night, so when he was approaching Wisbech and saw the signals against him, he blew on his whistle, making enough noise to wake up all the inhabitants. I was in the signal-box at Coldham waiting to catch the express to take me home, and when we heard the whistle the signalman on duty, Walter Barrett, said to me:

'I bet that's Peter Jackson.' He telephoned to Wisbech to ask where the express was and was told it was four miles away. Peter kept on whistling so Walter said: 'I'll give him a run,' and drew out a Tablet and pulled his starter and home signals off. Peter came towards us and as he took the Tablet Walter shouted out to him:

'Don't let me down.'

'All right,' said Peter, 'leave it to me,' and he roared past us making the earth shake. Then the express came along and I boarded it, expecting to see Peter shunted at one of the stations through which we passed, but when we drew in at Magdalen Road Peter had already passed St Germans Siding and we had a clear run; he had done this with a little goods engine which only weighed fifty-five or sixty tons.

There was a close and affectionate relationship between many of the drivers I have known – Peter Jackson, Harry Dack, Jim Taylor and many others – and their steam engines. I have always admired such men and often I would have been without a fire in the signal-box if they had not given me a scuttleful of coal. They were skilled workers, and I have seen many a driver and fireman going round an engine, a hammer in one hand and a Leary Lamp in the the other, with a gale-force wind blowing and yet never letting the lamp blow out. This was an oil-filled can into which was inserted a wick to burn a naked flame. When the coal strike of 1929 was on, drivers and firemen had a rough time for all they had to burn were brickets and logs of wood, and I have known them have to wait in a station for ten minutes to get up steam.

Over fifty years ago there was a big fire in King's Lynn – I believe it was at the drapery stores of Jermans and Perry. Fire engines from all over the neighbourhood were sent to fight the blaze and the one from Wisbech was sent by the 1.30 a.m. Mail train, arrangements being made to give it top speed on the journey. Old Alf Newman, the signalman at Magdalen Road, often told me how the train came round the curve so fast that the fireman missed the Tablet and Alf had to spend half an hour looking for it. That train, he said, was the fastest he ever saw or wanted to see and it careered into Lynn at such a speed that it crashed into the buffer stops. Alf, incidentally, eventually went to live at Watlington, near King's Lynn, in a double-fronted house with a large garden which, to his surprise one day, his wife announced that she had bought. She had saved up the money by putting aside, for thirty years, every penny piece she received in change when she was shopping.

Now all the steam engines have gone. No more shall we see the fireman cleaning his fire with a pricker or perched up on the tender breaking coal. Drivers of today's diesels have a nice clean job, with padded seats to sit on and a heater for boiling their kettles instead of having to stand their tea-cans over the firebox to keep them hot.

War and Accidents

A vivid picture still remains in my mind of the preparations for the invasion of France in the Second World War. One weekend from the Saturday evening until the Monday morning, train-loads of tanks passed through Waldersea at half-hourly intervals, all bound for Norfolk. Each train, drawn by two engines, held from twelve to twenty giant tanks – a wonderful sight, but, as my old friend Jim Loughton remarked to me, one that meant death and destruction. Earlier in the war, when a Nazi invasion of England was feared, engines, coupled together in twos and threes, were brought each night from King's Lynn, Hunstanton and other coastal stations, to stand at March or Whitemoor, returning to the coast at six o'clock the next morning. Armoured trains, mounted with guns pointing in all directions, each manned by soldiers, frequently went through Coldham and Waldersea too, a sinister sight though we knew they were doubtless on practice runs.

A number of Italian prisoners of war were sent to work on farms round Waldersea or on the railway and for some time I had two of them helping me; they were good workers and we got on well together. They used to cook their macaroni on the stove in my hut, mixing it with olive oil, onions, lettuce, sage or apples. One day, after a heavy thunderstorm, they collected from the grass enough snails to fill a gallon tin, these they washed well, cooked, picked out from the shells, and then stewed with macaroni, oil, onions and sage. I must admit that they smelt good, but though I was offered some I could not bring myself to eat them, although my mate had some and said they were delicious.

Jack Merel, a grower who used to bring potatoes down to the yard to be loaded, was a tall, strong man, and one morning he picked up a full hundredweight sack and tossed it casually over the side of the truck saying to one of the prisoners:

'What do you think of that, Philip?' Philip walked over to another bag and, though he only weighed about half as much as Jack, threw it easily over into the truck. All the loaders watching gave him a cheer.

'You surprise me,' said Jack, and when he came down to the yard again he brought the Italian a bottle of beer.

Philip had been taken prisoner in Abyssinia and had, in fact, not been in Italy for eleven years. He used to talk to us about Abyssinia, describing how the women worked all day in the fields while the men spent their days in gambling and their nights in stealing whatever they could lay their hands on. This must have been where Philip learned to steal, because he could take things from right in front of us without our knowing he had done so.

One day a grower brought some tomatoes down to us in twelve-pound chip baskets.

'Lovely tomatoes,' Philip kept saying, so the man offered him a couple, but Philip would only accept one. I was in the truck all the time with John, the other Italian, and the grower stood by as we loaded, and not one of us saw Philip take any of the tomatoes. As soon as the grower had left, however, he put his hand down the front of his open-necked shirt and pulled out, one by one, about six pounds. I made him take them over to the truck and John, who had been in the police force in Italy, threatened to get him sent to prison. Poor Philip looked as though he was going to burst into tears, and I persuaded John to say nothing about the affair – perhaps the fright would teach his fellow-countryman a lesson.

One morning a big army staff car drove down into the yard and out of it climbed an officer who came over to me and told me that, for the next few weeks, I should be receiving daily supplies of petrol. In a day or two it started to arrive, ten trucks a day filled with four-gallon cans which we unloaded for the twenty soldiers, who had been sent down to help, to transport by lorries to a big dump in Needham Hall Chase in Friday Bridge. Here the cans were buried and guarded day and night by sentries. The cans arrived in the trucks with what the soldiers called *dunnage* – old sacks, bits of torn coats and jackets – packed round them. These pieces of cloth got soaked with petrol, as many of the cans leaked, and gave us a messy job when we had to collect them up and send them back to Salisbury Plain after the cans had been transferred to the lorries. I often used to wonder what would happen if, when we were shunting the old steam engine, a hot cinder fell on the dunnage. This petrol, by the way, was never used, and after the war it was carted back to us and we had the task of loading it up again and sending it away.

On June 2nd, 1944, only four days before D-Day, a tragic event occurred at Soham, six miles to the south-east of Ely. In the early hours of the morning an ammunition train was travelling along near the station when the driver, Ben Gimbert, noticed a bright flame coming from the first wagon. The train was made up of about fifty trucks each containing unfused bombs, and he knew that if only one of these exploded it would mean the whole train, together with several thousand inhabitants of Soham, being blown to pieces. He decided that the best, and indeed the only thing that he and his mate Jim Nightall could do, was to uncouple the wagon, get it away from the rest of the train and leave it in a cutting where the effects of any explosion would, to a certain extent, be lessened. This he managed to do, and he had just called the Soham signalman, Frank Bridges, to warn him to stop the Mail train due to pass shortly, when the bombs exploded. A huge crater was made in the middle of the track, the buildings of Soham station disappeared and the Station Hotel, together with many roofs, windows and other parts of buildings in the town were blown away.

Ben Gimbert was seriously injured and Jim Nightall and Frank Bridges were killed, but it was the courage of these three men which saved thousands of lives that early morning. I knew Ben well, and Frank, who was always called Sailor, was cousin to my son-in-law, and I remember wishing him luck when he applied for the job of signalman at Soham. Driver Gimbert received the George Medal and one was also awarded posthumously to Jim Nightall.

Another accident occurred in 1944 although this one did not involve explosives. At two o'clock one morning, when I was in bed and asleep, the Mail train went through Waldersea making such a loud noise that it shook the whole house and wakened me and my wife, but it went on travelling so we turned over and went off to sleep again. About five minutes later, however, there was a loud knocking on our front door and the sound of someone calling 'Arthur, Arthur'. I put my head out of the bedroom window and saw it was one of the King's Lynn guards.

'Come on down, Arty,' he shouted, 'we're off the road with the Mail.'

I stopped only to put on trousers and socks and then, grabbing a torch, ran to the signal-box where I saw Fred Garrod, another guard, trying to get inside. When he saw me coming along he dashed off to put detonators down to protect his train while I switched on and sent the six bells signal which means *Obstruction – Danger* in each direction to warn signalmen in other boxes that I was not to be given a train under any consideration.

For the next half-hour it was as if all Bedlam were let loose. I had no one to ask what exactly had happened, and all the time the telephone kept ringing with inquiries as to where the Mail was, had there been an accident, and was anyone hurt. Finally the guard returned with the driver and I learned what had occurred.

A fish van loaded with five tons of fish and attached to the rear of the Mail train had, it seemed, jumped the rails, keeping upright but with the wheels off the metals. No one was hurt but the train was lock-buffered, which meant it could not be moved so it had to be left on the line with a fireman to guard it.

From the signal-box I could not see where the Mail had stopped although it was a bright-starlit morning, but presently I heard her whistle and start up, so I was able to ring Control and say she was on her way. Presently three Inspectors arrived and I certainly was not sorry to see them.

When it was daylight I was able to see the damage caused by the derailed van which had smashed all the chairs and splintered all the sleepers along a three-quarter-mile length of track. Whole sleepers had been torn up and hurled over the up line, while the iron rods at the crossover points had been uprooted and were standing on end. But by eight o'clock there were a hundred men down, taking out the damaged chairs and sleepers and levelling up the new ones which soon arrived. Before mid-morning trains were again running, though slowly, over the new road. Everywhere had had to be cleaned down because the door of the fish van had burst open and plaice, mackerel and cod were strewn all over the track. We picked them up, washed the ashes off them and that night from nearly every house in the district came the smell of frying.

Another accident on the line caused the death of a very dear friend of mine. I was not on duty at the time and had been out to give some water to my chickens which were out on the stubble fields. As I passed the signal-box on my way home I heard the two bells which meant that the Fenman express had left Wisbech, four miles away. Three or four minutes later, when I had forgotten all about the train, it suddenly dawned on me that I had not seen her go by the house, so I looked out of the window and saw that she had just arrived at the home signal with steam blowing off and smoke beating down from her. Then I noticed that the driver and his mate had climbed down and were pulling something out from under the engine and just then the guard, whom I knew well, came running up to me shouting that they thought they had hit a man on the bridge about half a mile back – could he borrow my bicycle so he could go and find out.

I lent him the bicycle then went over to the signal-box, switched on and allowed the train to come up to the box so that it was protected by the signals. In a minute or two the guard came back and reported that it was as they had thought – the man was dead, so after taking down the names of the train's crew and the number of the engine I let the Fenman proceed on her journey and then telephoned to the Station-master and the police.

Presently I learned that the dead man was my old friend who had been on his way to work as a navvy on the drains. He had been taking a short cut up the railway line but, as he was a bit deaf, he had not heard the Fenman approaching so had been thrown by it on to the drain-bridge. His son arrived for work a few minutes later and it fell to me to tell him of his father's death.

The morning of July 22nd, 1952, was a perfect one, misty at first but getting hotter as the day wore on. At about a quarter past ten, after working in the goods yard, I went into my office to check the railway sacks and go through the warehouse book. I had not been there long when I heard the rings on the block bell which told me that the big passenger engine had left March on its way to Wisbech to work the 11.25 train from Wisbech to Cambridge. I knew it would be five or six minutes before I had the two bells signal to say that the engine had passed Coldham, so I did not put my gates across the line straight away but waited for three minutes, then left the office, closed the gates and pulled my signals off.

Not a single person was about and I had returned to the office when I heard the 'train on' bells from Coldham, a mile away. The engine always ran with its tender first and never failed to give a short whistle just before it got to the crossing. I heard it do this then, just as it was level with the signal-box, it gave a longer whistle and I heard the wheels skidding, so I rushed out thinking it had perhaps knocked someone over on a small crossing about two hundred yards from the box.

I looked up the track and at first glance everything seemed to be all right; then the driver and guard came hurring up pointing at something. I looked round again and there, in a hollow beside the track, lay what looked like a little bundle of clothes. I rushed over and found the two-year-old daughter of my neighbour, Mrs White. As I picked her up I was sure she was dead, but to my relief she gave a little whimper; she was covered with blood and near her forehead was a big hole which made me think her eye must be out till I saw it was a large cinder.

The driver took the little girl to her home so that I could telephone for the doctor who came from Wisbech within fifteen minutes. He attended to her then wrapped her in blankets, put her in his car on a pillow on the lap of one of the porters from Coldham and drove her to hospital. Twenty minutes later he came back and told her parents that she had to go immediately to a hospital in St Albans for a brain operation.

She was operated on and made a remarkable recovery. When she was able to come home she still had to attend Wisbech Hospital and to go to a London hospital every three months for the next two years, and then twice yearly for the following two; but now she is a fine young woman and I do not think she feels any ill effects from her accident.

No one knows exactly how she got on the track that day, but she had been chasing butterflies in the garden with her brother half an hour before and it is thought that she must have got through the wire fence. Although the driver was looking over the side of the engine he was not able to see her until he had passed the box, at which moment the wheel guard must have hit her and thrown her a distance of twelve yards. Her mother still relives the accident each July 22nd, but Sandra White must be almost the only person who has been hit by an engine travelling at fifty miles an hour and has survived.

A working life spent among engines, trucks and huge loads of heavy goods brings a risk of accidents and I have, myself, had some very lucky escapes. Once – it was only four days before Christmas I remember – when I was working at shunting at Downham during the sugar beet season, another shunter, Maurice Lake, and I had got a goods train ready to go to Magdalen Road and then on to Peterborough. Then the driver said he wanted water, which meant that he had to shunt across to the up line which already had a goods train from Cambridge shunting on it, so I told the driver of this to stay where he was, clear of the crossover points, while the other driver came over to get water. Maurice and I meanwhile stood between the two trains, one of them stationary and the other moving quite fast. It was pitch dark and pouring with rain so we had on our overcoats. Then something hit me and knocked me flat, and in falling I knocked Maurice flat as well. I heard him shout out and thought he must at least have had a limb knocked off, and he told me later that he thought the same must have happened to me, but we both escaped with cuts and bruises. Our hand-lamps were smashed, one of our shunting poles was run over and our trousers, overcoats and knees were torn; apparently the driver on the stationary goods train had seen a lamp swinging and had thought I was calling him forward, but I had been putting a brake up on the moving train and in doing so my lamp must have swung round.

On another occasion I stepped from behind a departing goods train just as an express was coming by; I knew it was due but was so engrossed in looking through some consignment notes that I had forgotten all about it. Luckily I managed to step back in time. Yet another near-escape occurred when I was attaching a horse box to a passenger train which had no corridor, so there was not much room for me to stand as the horse box backed on. I stood with the coupling in my hand when someone waved his lamp; the driver opened out and hit the box, but I managed to let go of the coupling and hang on to the draw bar, but I was dragged along down the siding.

Loading goods into trucks nearly brought me trouble on two occasions. One day, when I was on top of a tall load of hay spreading sheets over the bales, one of the bales moved and down I fell to the wagon floor, but I only winded myself. At another time, as I opened the door of a truck full of seed potatoes, three bags rolled down on to my head. It is a wonder that my neck was not broken, but it was only stiff for a few days.

Some Personal Opinions and Last Memories

Although in 1921, along with thousands of others, I became redundant for a time, this was not, as now, because the railways were declining but because railwaymen who had been called up for military service were returning to their old jobs. Many of the dismissed men, of course, found it difficult to find other work, but I was fortunate; I was single and had only myself to think of and having worked already on the land I was able to return to it.

The railways themselves were then making a profit – now they run at an ever-increasing loss and it is my own opinion that they began to decline as long ago as the twenties, when the four big groups – the London & North Eastern, the Great Western, the Southern, and the London, Midland & Scottish – were formed by combining the previous smaller companies. Until then each company did its best to get trade and all the workers did all they could to beat a rival company. The big market gardening firm of Harrison Brothers, for whom I worked before I went on the Great Eastern Railway in 1918, grew hundreds of tons of early potatoes, cabbages, lettuces, strawberries and other fruit which they always sent to their own market in Manchester. Although many of their farms adjoined St Germans Siding or Wiggenhall Siding, or lay half a mile from Magdalen Road Station, Harrisons' often loaded their produce at Terrington station on the old Midland & Great Northern line because the traffic got through much more quickly from there.

Every few months the traffic manager of the Great Eastern Railway would want to know why we were not getting all Harrisons' valuable traffic, and a canvasser would be sent down to Mr Harrison who would tell him that, although sending goods through Terrington meant that they had to travel six miles by road in horse-drawn vans, it was worth it because the Midland & Great Northern Railway got them to Manchester before we did. At once the Great Eastern freight trains would be altered to catch different connections and Harrisons' would send their produce to us. As time went by, however, things slipped back; fruit and vegetables began to miss the early markets so back Harrisons' went to the Midland & Great Northern.

In my early days special trains were run from King's Lynn to Norwich when there was a football match, and this always meant competition between the Great Eastern Railway and the Midland & Great Northern Railway, although the latter line was the more direct. The Great Eastern drivers, however, did their best to get their trains back to King's Lynn before their rivals, and the signalmen all along the route co-operated by doing all they could to ensure there was no delay. Drivers and signalmen on the Midland & Great Northern, of course, did the same, and all this competition meant that the public got a really good service.

I have already mentioned how often, when I was at Waldersea, we were given too few trucks and tarpaulin sheets for our loads, so that time and time again fruit farmers and potato growers had to take their produce back and bring it down again next day. This was really due to bad distribution but it was men like us, at the loading end, who got abuse from the customers. Hundreds of us could see that things could not go on like this for long and we knew that one day traffic would fall away.

There was no improvement with nationalization, when the railways became the People's Railway. Instead of fares being decreased to meet the competition from the buses, and instead of freight charges being kept well below road traffic charges, both kept on being increased so that customers were driven away. To my mind it is far better to have a train full of passengers paying five shillings each than one carrying only ten whose tickets have cost them each a pound. As the railways are already losing so much each year they could let the people who own them get a little more benefit out of them and so help, at the same time, to reduce the number of deaths and accidents, caused by the increase of road traffic, for which the railways are partly responsible.

My own private opinion is that hundreds of pounds have been lost and a great deal of trouble has been caused among railway staff by the introduction of the Bonus Scheme. In the first place this has meant employing far more clerks and sub-inspectors; time and motion men have been brought in, all at higher wages than those earned by the workmen, while the workers get £2 to £3 a week more for doing the same amount of work. This is, of course, fine for those who work under the Bonus Scheme, but there are thousands of railwaymen whose jobs do not come under it and who therefore have no chance of earning an extra shilling; yet they have to pay the same for their food, rent, clothing and so on. If *all* the workers had been given a little extra I think they would have been more satisfied and it would not have been necessary to take on additional and highly-paid staff.

The closing down of so many stations is another thing I view with disfavour. At Waldersea Siding and Coldham, to take but two examples, the loading of goods diminished considerably, but even then the yearly takings at each place paid my wages and those of the woman who looked after the crossing-gates at night, and there were still a few hundred pounds left over. Now the stations are closed to goods but both are, in effect, costing more to run and yet no money is coming into them at all.

The throwing out for scrap of big, comparatively new steam engines was, in my opinion, another waste of money. I know that diesels are cheaper to run, but I do not think the steam engines should have been disposed of so quickly. Many of them still had fifteen to twenty years more work in them and to my mind, if the diesels had been bought at first for the Main lines and the steamers used for the branch lines until they needed so much repair that they were uneconomic, a good deal of money could have been saved.

All the stations between Magdalen Road and Wisbech and between Wisbech and March are now closed for freight, and so are the lines to Wisbech Harbour and the line from Wisbech to Upwell. The huge coaling station which I saw built has been blown down and the enormous Tranship Shed at Whitemoor has been demolished. Now there are only two or three freight trains a day passing along this line whereas, a few years ago, there would have been twenty or more in addition to the special coal, pig iron, timber and other goods trains which ran frequently. Except for the Fenman and the train which takes the youngsters to school in Wisbech, not one train has more than half a dozen people in it, and most of these are railway staff. To go by train from March to Wisbech takes only nine or ten minutes; the buses take three-quarters of an hour. If fares were halved I believe the trains would pay.

I am not expressing these views just because I was made redundant but because the decline of the railways saddens me. The railway has treated me well, giving me a watch for forty-five years of service, a lump sum and a weekly redundancy payment until I reached the age of sixty-five; I was allowed to stay on in the railway house at Waldersea and was later given the chance to purchase it, an opportunity which I have recently taken.

We now have a main water supply at Waldersea Siding, but when I first came to live here we had to use cisterns for catching any rain water that fell. During a long dry spell we often ran out of water, so a supply was sent to us from Wisbech in old engine tenders which were put opposite the railway cottages so that the water could be run through canvas pipes into our cisterns. The water was not very clean – it sometimes had a dead bird in it or little, wriggling creatures – but as our cisterns already housed a few worms and snails we took no notice. Each house had a charcoal filter and once the water had passed through this it was as clear as gin.

Sometimes it took a few days for the tenders to come along with our supplies so, in the meantime, we would fill baths and buckets from wagons which came from Wisbech where they had been 'hollow-sheeted' by the tying of new tarpaulin sheets over the top with a shallow depression left in the centre. This was filled with water, so when the engine brought the wagon along we only had to fill our buckets and empty them into the cisterns. The water tasted strongly of tar from the sheets, but it seemed to do us no harm – certainly none of us down here at Waldersea ailed very much.

I have many happy memories of my life as a railwayman, when I worked with good mates and under some of the best of Stationmasters; Mr A. Jordan and Mr George Curzon, for example, Mr Barrie Creek, Mr Arthur Harris and Mr Joe Baylis – to all of whom I am grateful for all that they did for me. Among the men who worked with me at Waldersea was Jim Hood, now one of the oldest main-line passenger guards at March. He was a keen footballer, a good darts-player but, above all, a great card-player and one of the keenest gamblers I have ever known. If he could get anyone to play with him he would play cards all through his dinner hour, while on Boxing Days which, when I first knew him, were working days, he would be playing cards with the plate-layers and signal fitters from eight o'clock in the morning until four o'clock in the afternoon. I was sorry when he left Waldersea but we have kept in touch over the years and when I was still working the signals he never failed, as he went by on a train, to lean out and wave to me.

Another railwayman I knew well was George Wyer who was one of the four special guards, known as the Big Four, who lived at March and worked the trains to Manchester, London and Parkstone. George was a staunch Labour man – he was always called the Red Tie Guard because of the red necktie he always wore, on and off duty – and the sight of anyone reading a newspaper other than the *Daily Herald* had the same effect on him as the waving of a red duster in front of a bull.

One evening, when I was travelling home on the 5.42 p.m. train from March, I got into the guard's van with George and, as I thought he looked a bit upset, I asked him what sort of day he had had. He looked at me, muttered and ground his teeth and then launched into his tale. He had, apparently, worked his train to Cambridge and had been standing beside it on the platform watching a crowd of American tourists who had been visiting the Colleges. Presently four clergymen had come up to him and asked him who all those people were, and George had replied:

'American tourists who are visiting this beautiful country of ours and spending their money looking at God's wonderful works.'

'Bravo,' one of the parsons had replied, 'we need their money badly thanks to those terrible miners' (the miners were on strike at the time). At this remark George had flown into a terrible rage and shouted:

'Stop! Stop! . . . you who preach God's word. Those miners work six days a week in the dark bowels of the earth while you stay above ground and breathe pure air. I'm ashamed of you – you should be an agent of God but you're no more than an agent of the wicked old Devil. You're a wolf in sheep's clothing and Hell will be your doom.'

George told me that quite a crowd gathered round to listen to what he was saying:

'I soon enlightened them,' he said, 'and as a parting shot I told that parson that, unless it meant other people would be killed, I hoped his church would fall on him next time he climbed up into his pulpit to preach.'

Another railwayman I knew was Reg Kerry, a driver. He lived in Wisbech and had to be on duty at King's Lynn at six o'clock in the morning and, as there was no train or bus at that early hour to take him there, he used to cycle the eleven miles. One very foggy morning he was going along the road as usual, though he was riding rather fast as he was a bit late, and because it was so cold and raw he had his head well down. All at once he ran into something large and solid which threw him off his bicycle. Picking himself up he peered through the fog to see what he had hit and there in front of him was an elephant and, tied to it, a camel. Reg pinched himself to see if he was really awake. 'The camel stood sneering at me,' he told me, 'and the elephant swung its trunk to and fro and I really thought I was having a nightmare.' He had no idea what to do so he got on his bicycle and started off again, but he had not gone far when he met a man on horseback who called out to him: 'Have you seen an elephant and a camel as you came along?'

'I not only saw them,' said Reg, 'but they nearly knocked me into the dyke; if you're looking for them they're not far back along the road.'

It appeared that a circus which had been in King's Lynn was moving to Wisbech, but because one of the elephants had a painful foot it had not been able to keep up with the others.

One man with whom I worked on one occasion gave me, I remember, a great surprise when I discovered who he was. It was in the early nineteen thirties and I had been called out from my home to switch on my signals because a goods train had been derailed at Coldham and was blocking the up road. Just as I reached the box a man arrived to act as pilotman wearing, as it was raining, the regulation rubber clothing that is issued to guards and shunters. He was a complete stranger to me, but I greeted him with the words:

'Are you the pilotman, mate?'

'That's right,' he replied.

He left me a single-line working form and asked me to sign his which is the usual procedure then, as I had accepted the up passenger train from Wisbech, he went down to see that the points were securely clipped and that everything was in order. He rode on the engine from Waldersea to March and continued as pilotman until the track was cleared and normal working was resumed in mid-afternoon, when he collected the forms, shook hands with me, somewhat to my surprise, and said he was glad everything had worked out so well in the end. It was not until after he had gone that I learned that he was the assistant Yard Master at Whitemoor, Mr G. F. Fiennes, who later became General Manager of the Eastern and North-Eastern sections of British Railways.

Years ago the farmers and fruit growers round Waldersea and Friday Bridge seemed to be part of the railway for we saw them nearly every day. When I first came here Woodhouse Farm at Friday Bridge was owned by Mr William Flint; then it was taken over, on his retirement, by his son and now it is farmed by a grandson who has children of his own, so that since 1923 I have known four generations of that family. I knew Mr H. J. Ward, too, who had large farms at Friday Bridge and Newton; he was a well-known figure with his dark moustache and the cloth cap with a button on the top which he wore winter and summer, weekdays and Sundays. His land at Friday Bridge adjoined the railway siding yard; he used to grave his potatoes all along the side of the yard so that, when his men were riddling them, they could carry them from the grave over a long plank and straight into the loading trucks. Mr Ward used to call at the yard on most Saturday afternoons to have a chat, and whenever he walked over his fields he used to keep stopping to pull up dock roots or twitch grass and these he would carry over to the roadway and put in a bag to burn when he got to the headland. He is dead now but his farms are still carried on by his widow and his sons. I have known three generations, too, of the Scott family of farmers who always loaded here at Waldersea Siding.

Now all the busy little stations which, in my young days, loaded so much produce are no longer used for freight and it is probably only a matter of time before the stations from Magdalen Road to Coldham are closed altogether – even Wisbech may become a halt station. No more, then, shall we see crowds of people on the platforms waiting to go to the seaside, to the Mart at King's Lynn or to Wisbech Fair. No more do we see huge loads of potatoes, corn, sugar beet and fruit lined up to go on to the trucks, or big droves of cattle and flocks of sheep waiting in the pens to be loaded up. Even the railwaymen today look strange in their new uniforms which are so different from the green cord ones which were worn when I first went to Magdalen Road. I can remember there was a change in uniform when the London and North Eastern Railway came into being, for when I went to Coldham on April 10th, 1923, I was issued with one of the new ones and it was the first that had been seen on that station.

I have seen steam engines go and diesels arrive and I can recall the days when passenger trains on the branch lines were, for the most part, made up of composite coaches – that is ones with no corridors and no heaters. Passengers who wished to keep their feet warm in cold weather could, on payment of a small sum, have a foot warmer placed in their compartment. At all big stations a large copper was kept boiling and into it were placed galvanized iron tanks filled with water and each a foot wide, a foot and a half long and six inches deep. The porters, using thick rags to protect their hands, would lift out the tanks and place them on the carriage floors; at the end of the journey they would be taken away and replaced in the copper. Needless to say, these footwarmers were invariably coated with thick red rust.

Often one reads in the daily papers of goods being lost on the railway between the loading station and their destination. This, I know, does sometimes occur when the doors of as yet-unlabelled trucks or vans which are being transhipped at the Tranship Sheds are accidentally closed. The trucks are then thought to be empty and are shunted out with other empty ones. In my time the goods which, to my surprise, I have found on opening vans which I thought contained nothing, have included large consignments of bacon, American khaki cloth, empty fruit boxes, chocolates, cabbages, tinned fish and whale meat, cabbages and fruit trees.

There is a railway custom which has always rather puzzled me, and that is the one of keeping in signal-boxes – at least in those that I have known, a copy of the Bible. At Magdalen Road, Middle Drove, Emneth, Wisbech, Waldersea Siding and Coldham there always used to be a very big one with large print; a very old signalman once told me that it was a rule that there should be one in every box. I have heard several reasons given for the custom – some people have said it was because the General Manager of the old Great Eastern Railway in the last century was a very religious man; others have declared that the Bibles were kept handy in case there was a serious accident on the line so that any clergyman on the scene could read from them to the injured and dying. The Bible at Waldersea disappeared many years ago when the signal-

The Author leaving his signal box

box was repaired, while the one at Coldham was not seen after a change in signalmen long ago. Recently, however, a clerk at Wisbech told me that there is, or certainly was in 1965, one still kept on Downham station.

On several occasions during my forty-seven years on the railway I was offered promotion, but this would have meant moving to a bigger station so I always refused, for I preferred working in the country. I have never regretted my decision because now that I am retired I can still go on living at Waldersea Siding, where I worked for so long, amid the sights and country sounds I have known all my days. To many people life in this remote Fenland spot would be dull and intolerable, but I would not choose to live anywhere else in the world. I am among and near old friends and workmates and although my dear wife is now dead my son lives with me so I am not alone, while not so far away I have two married daughters and small grandson. I can walk about the fields and countryside I have known for years, I can work in my garden and with my poultry and I can count myself fortunate in that I have been able to return, part-time, to the mole-catching which I learned from my father when I was a boy. The years I spent as a railwayman were happy ones, though perhaps I am glad that I am not setting out on them at the present time when so many changes are taking place. Some of the modern generation may think it is time such changes occurred, but the old way of things suited me well and, looking back, I have no regrets for the time I spent as a Fenland railwayman.

The Author leaving his signal box

box was repaired, while the one at Coldham was not seen after a change in signalmen long ago. Recently, however, a clerk at Wisbech told me that there is, or certainly was in 1965, one still kept on Downham station.

On several occasions during my forty-seven years on the railway I was offered promotion, but this would have meant moving to a bigger station so I always refused, for I preferred working in the country. I have never regretted my decision because now that I am retired I can still go on living at Waldersea Siding, where I worked for so long, amid the sights and country sounds I have known all my days. To many people life in this remote Fenland spot would be dull and intolerable, but I would not choose to live anywhere else in the world. I am among and near old friends and workmates and although my dear wife is now dead my son lives with me so I am not alone, while not so far away I have two married daughters and small grandson. I can walk about the fields and countryside I have known for years, I can work in my garden and with my poultry and I can count myself fortunate in that I have been able to return, part-time, to the mole-catching which I learned from my father when I was a boy. The years I spent as a railwayman were happy ones, though perhaps I am glad that I am not setting out on them at the present time when so many changes are taking place. Some of the modern generation may think it is time such changes occurred, but the old way of things suited me well and, looking back, I have no regrets for the time I spent as a Fenland railwayman.

The O'Donnell Lectures

Charles James O'Donnell, born 1850, provided a bequest in 1935 for an annual lecture in the National University of Ireland on the history of Ireland since the time of Cromwell, with particular reference to the histories, since 1641, of old Irish families.

Established in 1957, the O'Donnell lectures were delivered more or less annually for thirty years. The series petered out in the 1980s due to lack of funds, but in 1998, the Senate was pleased to be able to revive the O'Donnell Lectures. It has been decided that from 1999 onwards an annual lecture will be presented in each of the NUI Constituent Universities, in rotation.

This lecture, 28th in the series, was also the first O'Donnell lecture to be delivered at National University of Ireland, Maynooth.

The lecture has been published with funds from the NUI Publications Scheme.

The full list of O'Donnell Lectures given is included on pages 26-27.

Colm Lennon

Colm Lennon is a graduate of the National University of Ireland, having completed his MA at University College Dublin and his PhD at Maynooth. He is a Senior Lecturer in the Department of Modern History at NUI, Maynooth. Among his publications are *Richard Stanihurst the Dubliner* (Dublin, 1981), *The lords of Dublin in the age of Reformation* (Dublin, 1989), *Sixteenth-century Ireland: the incomplete conquest* (Dublin, 1994) and *An Irish prisoner of conscience of the Tudor era: Archbishop Richard Creagh of Armagh, 1523 - 86* (Dublin, 2000). In addition he has written many articles on the history of early modern Dublin and on the Reformation and Counter-Reformation in Ireland. He has jointly edited collections of records of Dublin Corporation and Christ Church Cathedral, Dublin. He has been editor of the journal *Archivium Hibernicum* since 1990.

The urban patriciates of early modern Ireland: a case-study of Limerick

Two recent perspectives from either end of the early modern period may serve to throw into stronger relief the area of enquiry of this paper. The title of a set of essays on Catholics under the penal laws, Endurance and emergence, reflects the shift in accepted thinking on that subject.[1] The period of the eighteenth century witnessed the slow recovery of the Catholic community from the shock of exclusion from political power after the Williamite Wars. Among the contributors to the discussion was Dr David Dickson who, in a previous O'Donnell lecture, revisited the question of the rise of Catholic families to positions of commercial prominence at a time when they had lost control of municipal governance in the port-towns.[2] In his separating out of the elements of the problem, Dr Dickson included the factor of geographical divergence as an influence on commercial continuity. In towns such as Galway and Limerick, and to a lesser extent Cork, he contends, where Catholics remained in the majority and where guild restrictions were less stringent than in the eastern and southern ports, the old patrician families who had dominated civic life down to the early seventeenth century had descendants who were established as substantial merchants by the end of the eighteenth.[3] By that stage, moreover, there was at least a tentative community between Catholic and Protestant merchant interests in respect of business concerns and outlook.[4]

The port-towns of the south and west emerge as comprising a distinctive cultural zone in the sixteenth century in another recent essay, this one by Brendan Bradshaw on 'The Reformation in the cities: Cork, Limerick and Galway, 1534-1603'.[5] The historical context is shown to be the protectiveness of the urban patriciates in the region of their rich heritage of civic and religious artefact and achievement which state-sponsored innovation threatened to destroy. Although traditionally bastions of loyalty to the English administration set in Gaelic and gaelicised hinterlands, these boroughs witnessed a growing alienation of the elites

---

[1] T.P. Power and Kevin Whelan (ed.), Endurance and emergence: Catholics in Ireland in the eighteenth century (Dublin, 1990).

[2] David Dickson, 'Catholics and trade in eighteenth-century Ireland: an old debate revisited' in Power and Whelan (ed.), Endurance and emergence, pp 85-100.

[3] Ibid., pp 89-90.

[4] Ibid., p. 98.

[5] In John Bradley (ed.), Settlement and society in medieval Ireland: studies presented to Francis Xavier Martin, O.S.A. (Kilkenny, 1988), pp 445-76.

from the government's programme of religious reform. For one thing, the official stress on anglicisation in terms of personnel and evangelism cut across the burgeoning sense of civic identity of the townspeople which incorporated elements of cultural pluralism and sturdy self-reliance.[6] Furthermore a receptivity to intellectual trends from the continent through flourishing trade links helped to promote among the merchant communities pioneering educational advances and to produce a higher number of students to be trained abroad in seminaries and colleges by comparison with other regions.[7] The success of the Counter-Reformation in the cities, as highlighted by Dr Bradshaw, created the dilemma of clashing religious and political allegiances for the ruling elites, the insolubility of which was the major cause of their loss of power in urban government in the mid-seventeenth century.

In this case-study of Limerick I wish to explore the continuity from the ascendant patricians of the Tudor and earlier Stuart periods to the successful commercial, though politically excluded, class of the later Georgian era. Firstly we shall consider how generations of experience in the urban milieu forged among the prime citizens a reserve of civic awareness and expertise which could be drawn upon in times of adversity. In particular the manipulating of electoral politics and the careful management of resources in order to preserve municipal unity sharpened the instinct for survival of the older families. Of great significance, secondly, in this fostering of patrician rootedness was their system of social connection and intercourse which encompassed all of the major families such as the Arthurs, Creaghs, Sextons, Whites, Stackpoles and Roches, and Protestant as well as Catholic branches. Thirdly, among this self-aware and self-confident coterie which dominated urban life in Limerick from the late middle ages there came to flourish a vibrant sense of cultural identity. They established ownership not just of the physical features but also of the history and traditions of the city. Among the leading families were preserved, for example, the very chronicles, annals and documents upon which much of this paper is based.[8] Manifestations of the durability of this cultural achievement may be seen in the recurrence of long-established family names among migrant scholars in the Irish colleges on the continent, among clergy returning to Ireland in the later seventeenth and eighteenth centuries and among schoolmasters who were instrumental in training

---

[6] Brendan Bradshaw, 'The Reformation in the cities: Cork, Limerick and Galway, 1534-1603' in Bradley (ed.), Settlement and society, pp 458, 465-71.

[7] Ibid., pp 447, 469.

[8] The principal annalistic collections are : 'Arthur manuscripts' (B[ritish] L[ibrary], Add. MS 31,885): parts of this collection have been edited by Edward MacLysaght and John Ainsworth in N[orth] M[unster] A[ntiquarian] J[ournal], ii (1940), p. 47; vi (1950-1), pp 29-49, 65-82; vii (1953-7), pp 168-82, 4-10; viii (1958-9), pp 2-19, 79-87; ix (1962-5), pp 51-9, 113-16, 155-64 ; Richard Creagh, 'On the origins of the O'Neills and Creaghs', c. 1583 (T.C.D., MS 568, f. 61); 'Account of the origins of the Creagh family' (N.L.I., MS 4600); 'Chronicle of Limerick' in 'Sexton's notebook', c. 1635 (N.L.I., MS 16085), pp 35-94; 'White's annals of Limerick' (N[ational] L[ibrary] of I[reland], MS 2714).

up youth to study abroad. To some extent these features may be discerned in other Irish boroughs in the early modern period but there were particular circumstances in Limerick which helped the older patricians to play a part in the emergent New Town of the Georgian period. A keen appreciation of their historical legacy may have helped to shield the old burgher families from extinction.

One of my objectives is to investigate how the elite of Limerick marshalled its resources in order to present a facade of unity. Paradoxically, then, I begin by referring to an action which bespeaks divisiveness and sectarianism. According to the notebook of family and civic events kept by Edmund Sexton, the corpse of his grandfather, also called Edmund, was disinterred shortly after his burial in St Mary's cathedral, Limerick, in the mid-1550s during Queen Mary's reign.[9] The perpetrators were Alderman Christopher Creagh, Piers White, described as Sexton's brother[-in law] and Edward White, the organist in the cathedral. His right arm was cut off at the elbow and left in the tomb, while the rest of his body was hanged by the heels above the ceiling of the chancel of the cathedral. There it remained for three years, until, shortly after the entombment of Sexton's widow, Katherine Arthur, a fleeing felon, hiding himself above the church, discovered the corpse. A reinterment then took place at night. The younger Edmund Sexton asserted that this sacrilegious act 'was done for his religion' as his grandfather had embraced the Reformation.[10] Indeed in a letter to the Dublin government the younger Edmund went further and uttered the suspicion that Sexton's physician had been procured to 'bleed him to death' because he 'had received the gospel'.[11]

Apart from its cruelty and vindictiveness, this episode is notable for its uniqueness in the mid-Tudor urban milieu where patterns of endogamy were very strong,[12] and the causes may have been more complex than the grandson suggested. The participants were members of the tightly-knit group of leading Limerick families. At least one, Piers White, was a close relation of the dead man, and there was kinship between another, Christopher Creagh, and the family of Sexton's widow, Katherine Arthur.[13] Edmund Sexton's ethnic origin among the Gaelic population of Thomond was not an issue in the assault upon his body: the family of Creagh, for example, was very conscious of its origins

---

[9] 'Sexton's notebook', c. 1635 (N.L.I., MS 16085, p. 49).

[10] Ibid.

[11] Limerick MSS (N.L.I., PC, 875-9, 15/35): I am very grateful to the staff of the National Library of Ireland for facilitating my access to these records.

[12] See, for example, Colm Lennon, The lords of Dublin in the age of Reformation (Dublin, 1989), pp 78-83.

[13] Visitation certificate of Master Thomas Arthur (Dublin, Genealogical Office, MS 47, p. 19).

among the Gaelic O'Neills of Ulster.[14] The desecrators and the deceased shared a common political allegiance to the English administration in Ireland while priding themselves upon their belonging to a venerable municipality. Confessional divisions, while present among the patriciates in Irish cities in the later sixteenth century, were normally excluded from public discourse in the interests of civic order. What made Edmund Sexton so controversial a figure in mid-century Limerick was not so much his enthusiasm for Protestantism as his monopolising of the spoils of royal ecclesiastical policy in the form of most of the monastic properties in the Limerick area. Ever since his unprecedented intrusion into the mayoralty in 1536 under the direct patronage of Henry VIII, Sexton had elicited feelings of fierce resentment among the civic leaders who objected strenuously to the 'crafty means' by which he obtained royal favour and largesse.[15] In fact the legacy of contention lingered on into the seventeenth century: for much of his career, Edmund Sexton the younger was engaged in litigation with Limerick corporation over the rights to the extensive abbey lands which his ancestor had acquired.[16]

The success of urban communities in maintaining municipal stability and integrity depended upon the socio-political harmony of the elite governing class. Comprising about two dozen mercantile families, the ascendant coterie in Limerick displayed remarkable resilience in the face of political, economic and religious change for much of the early modern period.17 Social cohesion was attained through the careful ritualising of the civic *cursus honorum*, the shepherding of wealth and property through investment and partnership, the induction of well-disposed newcomers and the creation of close ties of affinity through intermarriage within the order. Concomitantly, the role of the members as cultural cynosures through their patronage of education, learning and piety served to forge an image for the city and its ruling oligarchy. All of the families represented in the events of the mid-1550s and its sequel - the Sextons, Whites, Arthurs and Creaghs - preserved either cartularies, annals, civic chronicles, family business and genealogical records or scholarly tracts.18

---

[14] See Richard Creagh, 'On the origins of the O'Neills and Creaghs', c. 1583 (T.C.D., MS 568, f. 61); for an account of Edmund Sexton's background, see Maurice Lenihan, Limerick: its history and antiquity (Dublin, 1866), pp 80-4, 86-7, and see also 'Sexton's notebook', c. 1635, s.a. 1485, 1535 (N.L.I., MS 16085, p. 44).

[15] Cf. L. & P. Hen.VIII, xiii, pt 2, pp 932, 1032; Brendan Bradshaw, The dissolution of the religious orders in Ireland under Henry VIII (Cambridge, 1974), pp 80, 102-3, 148-9.

[16] See, for example, Papers relating to the Sexton family (B.L., Add. MS 19865), pp 91, 92-6, 101-2, 105-6, 113-19; Limerick MSS (N.L.I., PC, 875-9),15/30, 31, 35, 47; 19/ 2f; 21/2; 25/31.

[17] The composition of the civic elite of Limerick is derived primarily from the lists of mayors and bailiffs of the city from c.1550 to c.1650: see John Ferrar, History of Limerick (Limerick, 1767), pp 127-35.

[18] See note 8, above.

And all produced formidable figures for positions of leadership in the professional, political and ecclesiastical spheres in Limerick: the aforementioned Edmund Sextons, Dr Dominic White, Dr Thomas Arthur and Primate Richard Creagh.[19]

In a very real sense the Limerick which emerged from the middle ages was the creation of the patriciate. In today's city the names of the old families are still preserved in such urban features as Creagh Lane, Arthur's Quay, Sexton Street, Roche's Street and White's Lane, and Roche's Stores have a national profile.[20] Topographical identity, conferred first in the prose accounts of natives such as David Wolfe and Edmund Sexton in the sixteenth century[21], was crystallised in the earliest maps of the city with its signature hour-glass shape.[22] By the seventeenth century the old dualistic structure of Englishtown and Irishtown had little or no political or racial significance, and this conjoint entity was the framework for urban life until the famous walls were removed in mid-eighteenth century.[23] Within this ambit and its immediate hinterland the traces of the building activity of the older elite were everywhere evident as Thomas Dineley discovered when he visited Limerick in 1680-1. Although by that time they had been ousted from municipal government, the older families were commemorated in a whole series of plaques in public places, dutifully recorded by the English visitor. The name of Piers Creagh FitzAndrew, an energetic improver, appeared on several of these, as did those of members of the Roche, Comyn, Fanning, Rice and Sexton families.[24] An important example of familial survival was embodied in the large Creagh House in Broad Street in Irishtown in the later eighteenth century. John Creagh re-edified the buildings erected by his ancestor, Peter Creagh, and had inscribed on a tablet in a new archway: 'Built in 1640 By Pierce Creagh Re built 1767 by John Creagh'.[25]

---

[19] For a synopsis of Edmund Sexton the elder's career, see Lenihan, Limerick, pp 80-91; the career of Edmund the younger (1569-1636) may be reconstructed from 'Sexton's notebook', c. 1635 (N.L.I., MS 16085), pp 35-94; for Dominic White, see 'White's annals of Limerick' (N.L.I., MS 2714), p. 58; and a notice of Thomas Arthur is contained in John Widdess, 'A notable Irish physician: Dr Thomas Arthur, 1593-1675' in Irish Journal of Medical Science (1957), pp 21-31; for Richard Creagh, see Colm Lennon, An Irish prisoner of conscience of the Tudor era: Archbishop Richard Creagh of Armagh, 1523-86 (Dublin, 2000).

[20] See Gerry Joyce, Limerick street-names (Limerick, 1995).

[21] For Wolfe's account, see 'Father Wolfe's description of Limerick, 1574', ed. Brendan Bradshaw, in N.M.A.J., xvii (1975), pp 47-53, and for Sexton's, see Papers relating to the Sexton family (B.L., Add. MS 19865), pp 69-72.

[22] The earliest map was drawn about 1590, and that of John Speed appeared in 1611: see Judith Hill, The building of Limerick (Cork, 1997), pp 26-7.

[23] See P.J. O'Connor, Exploring Limerick's past: an historical geography of urban development in county and city (Newcastlewest, 1987), pp 36-50; Hill, Building of Limerick, pp 58-90.

[24] For Dineley's account of his visit to Limerick, see 'Extracts from the journal of Thomas Dineley, esquire', edited by Maurice Lenihan, in Journal of the Kilkenny and south-east of Ireland Archaeological Society, v (1866), pp 425-46.

[25] Lenihan, Limerick, p. 357.

Their awareness of the antiquity of municipal traditions in Limerick is attested by the preservation of charters and urban chronicles by leading families. The Sexton family papers include copies of Tudor and Stuart charters,[26] and the annals of the White family, compiled in the eighteenth century, contain a listing of the mayors, bailiffs and sheriffs of the city from 1198 and of the chartered privileges bestowed by the English monarchy.[27] This self-conscious determination to present themselves, the inheritors of generations of urban sophistication, as a historical community was no doubt piqued by the political challenges of the seventeenth century. As they saw it, it was under the aegis of the patrician cohort that full borough status for Limerick was attained in 1609, and it was through conciliar solidarity that civic progress and independence could be maintained. Thus, for example, there were strict laws governing membership of the panel of householders from which the civic council was elected. Although couched in racially exclusivist rhetoric, the regulations of 1512 for the admission to the panel of those who could 'speak English and be well clothed in English apparel' were primarily concerned with the integrity of urban life and the ascendancy of its ruling group which accommodated some of Gaelic background such as the Sextons and Creaghs.[28] It was this coterie which attracted royal patronage in the early modern period through the granting by charter of the trappings and symbols of devolved power. Queen Elizabeth bestowed a sword to be borne before the mayor by a swordbearer wearing the cap of maintenance.[29] The ceremonial riding of the franchises by the mayor and his party of civic dignitaries was given added point by the extension of the city's vicinage from a circumference of one to three miles in the 1609 charter of James I.[30] This culminating accolade of civic loyalty awarded county borough status to Limerick city, its bailiffs being raised to sheriffs and the fulness of municipal power being vested in the named urban magnates.

This power they retained until the 1650s when the Cromwellian regime appointed twelve English aldermen to replace those of the older patrician families, but the latter left a legacy of inurement in political and diplomatic manoeuvring as they withdrew from active civic governance. The careful maintenance of an orderly succession to the highest corporation offices of mayor and sheriff through strict adherence to seniority had come under severe pressure during the period known

---

[26] See, for example, Limerick MSS (N.L.I., PC, 875-9), 15/71,75, 21/1.

[27] 'White's annals of Limerick' (N.L.I., MS 2714), pp 3-17, 43, 45-53.

[28] P. Fitzgerald and J.J. McGregor, <u>The history, topography and antiquities of the county and city of Limerick</u> (2 vols, Dublin, 1826-7), ii, p. 410.

[29] Robert Herbert, 'The antiquities of the corporation of Limerick' in <u>N.M.A.J.</u>, iv (1944-5), p. 93.

[30] Ibid., p. 95: the text of the charter of 1609 is transcribed in 'Papers relating to the Sexton family' (B.L., Add. MS 19865), pp 145ff.

as 'the battle of the mayors' from 1605 to 1616.[31] A whole series of debarments from office of elected mayors and sheriffs resulted from the imposition of the oath of supremacy by the Munster president but civic government was held together by the juggling of the principal offices among those eligible.[32] These included well-connected Protestants such as Edmund Sexton who was advanced to the mayoralty for an unprecedented four times. He claimed that this was done by the corporation leaders 'to save themselves and to excuse their obstinacy'.[33] But Limerick managed to retain its cherished chartered liberties at a time when, for instance, the city of Waterford lost its charter due to patrician 'obstinacy' in the face of government policies.[34] Two chief governors, Lord Falkland and Thomas Wentworth, were sumptuously entertained in Limerick in the 1620s and 1630s at the houses of Edmund Sexton and Dr Dominic White respectively.[35] During the greatest test of civic solidarity in the 1640s, underlying tensions on the Catholic confederate side boiled over on the famous 'stony Thursday' when Mayor John Bourke was forced from office in a coup led by Dominic Fanning in 1646.[36] Yet a variety of stratagems was deployed to preserve Limerick's standing and independence, including the pressing of the city's most famous person, Dr Thomas Arthur, to serve as intermediary with the confederates.[37] The surrender to Ireton in 1651 ended this phase of patrician ascendancy but it is significant that in 1687 when another revolution in civic politics occurred under James II the membership of the bench of aldermen contained several family names which appear on the list of senior city councillors in 1609 and 1643.[38]

As in the other Irish boroughs, there was a high level of interchangeability between senior office-holders in Limerick and those who dominated the

---

[31] Liam Irwin, 'Seventeenth-century Limerick' in David Lee (ed.), Remembering Limerick: historical essays celebrating the eight hundredth anniversary of Limerick's first charter granted in 1197 (Limerick, 1997), pp 114-22.

[32] John Begley, The diocese of Limerick in the sixteenth and seventeenth centuries (Dublin, 1927), pp 294-301.

[33] Limerick MSS (N.L.I., PC, 875-9), 15/35.

[34] Aidan Clarke, 'Plantation and the Catholic question, 1603-23' in T.W. Moody, F.X. Martin and F.J. Byrne (ed.), A new history of Ireland, iii: early modern Ireland, 1534-1691 (Oxford, 1976), p. 224.

[35] Begley, Diocese of Limerick in the sixteenth and seventeenth centuries, pp 302-3; 'White's annals of Limerick' (N.L.I., MS 2714), p. 60.

[36] Irwin, 'Seventeenth-century Limerick', pp 116-18; for a discussion of the political context, see Eamon O'Flaherty, 'The urban community and the state, 1590-1690' in Bernadette Whelan (ed.), The last of the great wars: essays on the war of the three kings in Ireland, 1688-91 (Limerick, 1995), pp 171-6.

[37] Irwin, 'Seventeenth-century Limerick', p. 117.

[38] Lenihan, Limerick, p. 272; see below, Figure 1.

long-distance trade of the port. Commensurate with their experience in the political sphere, the Limerick mercantile families had been called upon to display adaptability in the face of a variety of challenges. There was a long history of piracy and privateering along the shipping routes between southern Ireland and the continent and Britain. In 1428, for example, the ship and cargo of Nicholas Arthur of Limerick had been seized by Breton pirates and he himself imprisoned for two years on Mont St-Michel.[39] Lords of lands along the Shannon estuary regularly engaged in forestalling the city markets and exacting heavy tribute from the merchant fleet.[40] Serious clashes took place between the merchant communities of Limerick and Galway over supremacy in the trade of the west coast.[41] The resilience of the Limerick merchants is evident both in self-reliance and in recourse to the crown for assistance in protecting their commerce. In 1505 a 'great tri-oared galley fitted out with all things necessary' had been launched to patrol the river and sea-lanes.[42] The fortification of Scattery Island by some of their number in an attempt to control traffic through the mouth of the estuary was formalised by Queen Elizabeth in 1578 with the grant to the city of the former monastic site of St Senan.[43] The corporation of Limerick continued to claim these chartered rights to the island and the associated customs levy of oysters and herrings down to the later eighteenth century.[44] Royal intervention stemmed the fierce competition with the port of Galway after a trade war in the 1520s, and the market of the Limerick merchants was upheld in a letter of Henry VIII of 1536.[45] The Elizabethan and early Stuart charters were designed to bolster the economic position of Limerick as much as they were to enhance its political standing.[46]

Despite the upheavals of the late seventeenth century with which Limerick was to become synonymous, a coterie of older patrician families displayed remarkable tenacity in the commercial sector. In this respect the city was advantaged by the maritime and municipal legacy of the late middle ages. Limerick's flourishing regional and overseas trading networks provided reciprocating systems for commercial and social success especially in straitened domestic economic circumstances.[47]

---

[39] Timothy O'Neill, Merchants and mariners in medieval Ireland (Dublin, 1987), p. 128.

[40] Lenihan, Limerick, p. 91.

[41] Fitzgerald and McGregor, History, topography and antiquities of Limerick, ii, p. 400.

[42] O'Neill, Merchants and mariners, p. 128.

[43] For a transcription of this grant, see Papers relating to the Sexton family (B.L., Add. MS 19865), p. 69.

[44] See, for example, 'White's annals of Limerick' (N.L.I., MS 2714), p. 69.

[45] Fitzgerald and McGregor, History, topography and antiquities of Limerick, ii, pp 411-13.

[46] For a discussion of the mercantilist context for English policy towards Irish boroughs, see Colm Lennon, The lords of Dublin in the age of Reformation (Dublin, 1989), pp 104-6.

[47] Louis Cullen, The emergence of modern Ireland, 1600-1900 (London, 1981), pp 117-20.

The existence of such a nexus is attested, for example, by Richard Creagh who, as he set out on his ill-fated episcopal mission to Armagh in the mid-1560s, made arrangements for postal communications with southern Europe through the agency of Limerick merchants in Cadiz.[48] A century later, another Richard Creagh was a leading banker and merchant in La Rochelle, one of a large community of emigrés from Limerick settled in the Atlantic ports of France.[49] Much nearer home, the mercantile community of Ennis in the seventeenth and eighteenth centuries had at least a dozen families which had branches in Limerick.[50] Within the municipality, their exclusion from the guilds was a concomitant of the loss of political power after the 1650s, but the effects on the older patricians were mitigated by the disassociation of the economic and civic functions of these institutions. Thus, for example, disputes over quarterage were less intensive in Limerick than elsewhere.[51] The old mercantile elite had been shielded from internal commercial competition until later than in other boroughs as comparatively few new English or continental merchants set up in Limerick before the 1650s. At the time of the Civil Survey in 1654 only 5% of city property-owners were Protestant (this minority including the Sextons) but by 1659, the Census recorded that 53% were Protestant, most of the names listed being those of newcomers.[52] Yet some of the major trading families succeeded in maintaining their commercial hold to judge by the listings in a Limerick trade directory of 1769. Among those with premises on the Main Streets of Englishtown and Irishtown were Patrick and Joseph Arthur, James and William Creagh, William and Patrick Bourke, Stephen and Philip Roche, Michael and Helena Stritch, Thomas Harrold and William White.[53]

Dominating the political and economic life of the city, members of the long-established elite were associates in an honorific estate to which were due public esteem and deference. In fostering their ruling style, they cultivated their own genealogical roots and actively forged social solidarity. The leading families displayed their interest in tracing their pedigrees to antiquity. Among the voluminous manuscripts of Dr Thomas Arthur is his account of his family, tracing the name of Arthur from the writings of Juvenal and mentioning its connection with the constellation Bootes, Arcturus.[54] Medieval references culminate in the arrival of the Norman bearer of the name in Limerick from whose time the heads

---

[48] Richard Creagh to Juan de Polanco, Madrid, 28 April 1566 (Archivium Romanum Societatis Iesu, Epistolae Externorum, 10, f. 275).

[49] Inventaire sommaire des Archives Departementes anterieures a 1790: Charente Inferieure (La Rochelle, 1900), p. 239: I am very grateful to Dr Marian Lyons for this reference.

[50] See Sean Spellissy, The merchants of Ennis (Cork, n.d.).

[51] Dickson, 'Catholics and trade in eighteenth-century Ireland', p. 89.

[52] O'Connor, Exploring Limerick's past, pp 36-40.

[53] John Ferrar, Limerick Directory (Limerick, 1769).

[54] See Lenihan, Limerick, pp 367-9

of the family and their spouses down through several generations are listed.[55] Richard Creagh traced his forebears back through seven generations to the family's first arrival in the Limerick area and thence to the patrilineal Craidhan O'Neill of Lifford. As he lay incarcerated in the Tower of London, Creagh arranged for the drawing up of the family coat of arms, noting with pride that a version of the Creagh crest was embossed upon their tomb in the ancestral chapel in St Mary's cathedral which was in itself was a heraldic monument to Limerick's elite.[56] Besides the Arthurs and Creaghs, the Sextons and Whites were among the families who had appointed chapels in their memories in the hallowed spot.[57] Both also had an acute awareness of their family's place in Limerick history. Edmund Sexton junior interwove the milestones in his own family's ascent with his chronicle of urban events, noting dates of births, marriages and deaths therein.[58] The eighteenth-century annalist, Rev. James White, gave expression to *pietas* in recording in his annals that William Lysaght, sheriff in 1637, was 'great-grandfather to this compiler'.[59]

Individual families cherished their past in the form of heraldry and genealogy, and they preserved their status and property in the present through their matrimonial ties. As with other Irish boroughs, members of the colonial elite of Limerick had a small pool of potential partners to draw upon. Dispensations for marriage within the close degrees of consanguinity were common as in the case of Nicholas Arthur who was doubly related to his bride within the fourth degree,[60] and Leonard Creagh and his wife, Joan White, who were of the same kin.[61] Indeed Primate Richard Creagh professed his belief in the 1560s that the Tridentine decrees on marriage would be impossible to enforce in his native Limerick as eligible partners were strictly limited for urban women such as his sister for whom it would be very shameful to marry a social inferior.[62] Thus the patrician families intermarried with the urban elites of other Munster towns such as Cork and Clonmel. The pattern of nuptiality, anchored by the four leading families of Arthur, Creagh, Sexton and

---

[55] See 'The fee book of a physician of the seventeenth century', ed. Maurice Lenihan in Journal of the Kilkenny and south-east of Ireland Archaeological Society, vi (1867), pp 17-20; 'The Arthur Manuscript', ed. MacLysaght and Ainsworth in N. M. A. J., ix (1965), pp 155-64.

[56] Richard Creagh, 'On the origins of the O'Neills and Creaghs', c. 1583 (T.C.D., MS 568), f. 61.

[57] For information on the altars and chapels of St Mary's cathedral, see R.F. Hewson, 'St Mary's cathedral, Limerick: its development and growth' in N. M. A. J., iv (1944), pp 55-67; see also Dineley's account in 'Journal of Thomas Dineley', edited by Lenihan, in Journal of the Kilkenny and south-east of Ireland Archaeological Society, v (1866), pp 431-8.

[58] 'Chronicle of Limerick' in 'Sexton's notebook', c. 1635 (N.L.I., MS 16085), pp 35-94.

[59] 'White's annals of Limerick' (N.L.I., MS 2714), p. 60.

[60] Lenihan, Limerick, p. 366n [check]: Arthur and his wife received a papal dispensation permitting their marriage in 1426.

[61] 'White's annals of Limerick' (N.L.I., MS 2714), p. 59.

[62] Richard Creagh to Juan de Polanco, Madrid, 28 April 1566 (Archivium Romanum Societatis Iesu, Epistolae Externorum, 10, f. 275).

White, shows that the marital connections within this closely-knit endogamous society encompassed most of the leading families.[63] The main kin-groups are multiply matched over the century and half between 1500 and 1650, and the induction of newcomers from outside the region and from the Gaelic world was managed strategically. Even though, as we shall see, the Pery-Sexton alliance was of immense importance as a conduit for the development of Limerick and its older families, the Sexton connection in the early seventeenth century kept itself somewhat aloof from the civic mainstream. For example, in his records of the birth of his seventeen children, Edmund Sexton junior listed the godparents at their christenings and all belonged to the very small Protestant community of the city.[64] Generally, however, the tight bonds of affinity brought greater social unity and stronger resilience at a time of a massive incursus of newcomers after 1650s.

The social ascendancy of the old Limerick patrician families was bolstered by their research into the antiquity and superiority of their lineages. This sense of themselves as an elite is reflected in the family chronicles and genealogies, and also in the plaques and crests commemorating their building projects and the burial places of their ancestry. There were up to a dozen chantries established in chapels in St Mary's cathedral in the century before the Reformation bearing the names of leading families, and some of these continued in use long afterwards.[65] Secular and religious patronage on the part of the wealthy gave expression to piety and also to a collective feeling of communal worth. In an ecclesiastical setting the beautiful misericords in St Mary's cathedral, the finest of their kind in the country, were the fruit of lavish patronage of sculpture before the Reformation.[66] A distinctive urban identity began to be projected, not just in bye-laws restricting entry to the panel of householders, but in the presentation of Limerick's civic history as incorporating both Viking and Norman strains.[67] Nor did the Reformation cause a great fracturing of the civic psyche, the violent incident of the 1550s notwithstanding. Perhaps for essentially political and economic reasons the unity of the governing class held firm until the 1640s, the few Protestants or newcomer families subscribing to the predominant municipal if not the religious ethos. Despite the putative attraction of its English vernacular medium, the Reformation failed to appeal to more than a small minority of the anglophone townsfolk. By contrast, the Counter-Reformation which took hold in the city by

---

[63] See Figure 2.

[64] 'Sexton's notebook', c. 1635 (N.L.I., MS 16085), pp 142-3.

[65] R.F. Hewson, 'St Mary's cathedral, Limerick: its development and growth' in N. M. A. J., iv (1944), pp 55-67; see 'Sexton's notebook', c. 1635 (N.L.I., MS 16085), p. 90, for a reference to the repair of the Sexton and Creagh chapels in 1631.

[66] J.A. Haydn, Misericords in St Mary's cathedral, Limerick, revised by M.J. Talbot (Limerick, 1994).

[67] 'White's annals of Limerick' (N.L.I., MS 2714), pp 2, 26-7, 41-3.

the seventeenth century incorporated a Gaelic-speaking strand which rooted the movement more firmly in the region and highlighted Limerick's relations with its Gaelic hinterland.[68]

The community supported important educational advances which formed the basis of the intellectual flowering of Limerick in the seventeenth century. About 1557 Richard Creagh opened a grammar school in the former Dominican priory in the city and was joined as master there by Thomas Leverous, the deprived bishop of Meath, after 1558.[69] A priest who had changed his career path from that of merchant to scholar at Louvain, Creagh was a pioneer of Irish pedagogy, campaigning for second- and third-level academies to be established throughout the island. His own scholarly contributions to curricular studies included a scientific treatise on the Irish language, an Irish hagiography and, most significantly, a bilingual catechism in Irish and English, 'Epitome officii hominis Christiani'.[70] Through his advocacy, the first Irish Jesuit school was founded in Limerick in the 1560s, run by Edmund Daniel and William Good.[71] In spite of some discontinuity, a visitor in 1590 observed 'one hundred and three schollers, most of them speaking good and perfect English, for that they used to conster the Latin into English'.[72] By 1615, royal commissioners found that a popish schoolmaster, one Arthur, taught a public school in Limerick and had a great attendance of scholars.[73] The products of this academic milieu raised the scholastic profile of the city in Ireland and abroad. Half of the ten-strong Jesuit mission to Ireland in the mid-sixteenth century, including Edmund Daniel and David Wolfe, were natives of Limerick.[74] Over the following two centuries large numbers of students migrated to centres of learning on the continent, joining the diaspora of Limerick people and some returning to work as priests in the diocese.

A thriving literary and cultural milieu emanated from these educational advances in seventeenth-century Limerick. Perhaps the atmosphere alluded to by Luke Gernon, a contemporary visitor, was germane: 'The High Streete is builte from one gate to the other in one forme, like the colleges in Oxford, so magnificent that at my first entrance it did amaze me'.[75] While of intrinsic aesthetic value in itself, the more significant aspect of this flowering lies perhaps in its conferring intellectual substantiality on the patriciate's holding. The libraries of the leading families such

---

[68] Bradshaw, 'The Reformation in the cities' in Bradley (ed.), Settlement and society, pp 465-71.

[69] Lennon, An Irish prisoner of conscience of the Tudor era, pp 43-5.

[70] Ibid., pp 135-7.

[71] Proinnsias O Fionnagáin, The Jesuit missions to Ireland (Dublin, 1978), pp 19-23.

[72] Timothy Corcoran (ed.), State papers in Irish education (Dublin, 1916), pp 55-6.

[73] Begley, Diocese of Limerick in the sixteenth and seventeenth centuries, p. 396.

[74] O Fionnagáin, The Jesuit missions to Ireland.

[75] Cited in Hill, The building of Limerick, p. 29.

as Sexton and Arthur contained not only rich documentation of their claims to a stake in the city but also incorporated impressive collections of books. A 1630 catalogue of Edmund Sexton's 130 books, inherited by his son, Christopher, lists fifty-two works of theology and devotion, as well as volumes on history, husbandry, medicine, grammar and law.[76] Dr Thomas Arthur, his contemporary, possessed over 270 books, most of them devoted to medicine and the remainder on logic, history, theology and literature.[77] Sexton, a staunch Protestant who had inherited some of his grandfather's books, had been educated in Oxford and London.[78] Arthur, by contrast, who had qualified in medicine at Rheims, was a Catholic but his extensive case-book contained the names of leading dignitaries of church and state, including Archbishop James Ussher and Lady Chichester, as well as members of the principal Limerick families.[79] Arthur bridged the confessional divide through his literary relations with two primates, James Ussher and Richard Creagh. Through his friendship with Ussher he had access to the polymath's collections of lives of the Irish saints which he collated in his own edition, and he was literary executor to Creagh, his fellow-Limerickman and kinsman, transmitting to his descendants some of Creagh's writings including the important catechism.[80]

Patronage of the church continued among the Limerick patrician families after the Reformation. For the Catholic majority the old places of worship were no longer theirs for the demonstration of the piety and for interment, though some continuity in burial patterns is evident in the buying by leading citizens of grave plots in St John's church from the new impropriator, Edmund Sexton.[81] Donation to the church took the form of individual offerings such as the splendid Arthur cross which was made at the instance of Bishop Richard Arthur with the beneficence of Jane Fox, a widow, James Lange and others.[82] It is a large plate-gilt crucifix, hollowed out to contain a piece of the true cross. Leonard Creagh and Joan White bestowed a silver chalice on the restored Franciscan community of Limerick in

---

[76] Papers relating to the Sexton family (B.L., Add. MS 19865), ff 74-8: I am very grateful to Dr Raymond Gillespie for providing me with a transcript of the list of books.

[77] 'The Arthur Manuscript', ed. MacLysaght and Ainsworth in N. M. A. J., viii (1959), pp 79-87.

[78] 'Sexton's notebook', c. 1635 (N.L.I., MS 16085), pp 49-50.

[79] 'The fee book of a physician of the seventeenth century', ed. Maurice Lenihan in Journal of the Kilkenny and south-east of Ireland Archaeological Society, vi (1867), pp 10-33.

[80] 'Lives of Irish saints copied from books in the possession of Dr Thomas Arthur, James Ussher, 1627' (Maynooth, MS 3 G 1); Lennon, An Irish prisoner of conscience of the Tudor era, p. 135; Lenihan, Limerick, p. 119.

[81] Limerick MSS (N.L.I., PC 875-9), 24/5; in 1607, after his execution as a traitor, John Bourke of Brittas (who was later accounted a martyr among the Catholic community) was buried in St John's, Limerick: David Rothe, De processu martyriali quorundam fidei pugilum in Hibernia (Cologne, 1619), p. 181.

[82] J. Hunt, 'The Arthur cross' in Journal of the Royal Society of Antiquaries of Ireland, lxxxv (1955), pp 84-8.

1627.[83] Charitable provision for the poor and sick continued through the period from the Reformation. In the 1560s Helen Stackpole had founded an order called the Mena Bochta which ministered to the street women of the city.[84] The stone plaque erected in the front wall of the newly-built St John's hospital in 1651 attests the patronage of Alderman John Creagh.[85] An example of private patronage of Limerick craftware is the splendid delft bowl made in 1761 by the delphmaker, John Stritch, for Edmond Sexton Pery, whose initials are inscribed on the base.[86]

This sponsorship by the leading citizen of the mid-eighteenth century Limerick of a Catholic craftsman draws our attention to a vital confluence of interests concentrated on the family of Sexton Pery. An embodiment of this is the great collection of manuscripts, spanning the fifteenth to the nineteenth centuries, which surely comprises one of the most impressive documentary records of Irish familial continuity, excepting perhaps the great earldoms of Ormond and Kildare.[87] The story of how the foundations laid by the contentious Edmund Sexton senior in the mid-sixteenth century were built upon for magnificent urban development and indeed Catholic commercial renaissance during the career of his great-great-grandson, Edmund Sexton Pery, in the later eighteenth is a suitable synthesising of the elements discussed in this paper. In many ways, Edmund Sexton junior who died in 1636 is the unlikely pivotal figure. Besides his chronicling of family and civic events, Edmund formed an archive of his 'evidences' - deeds, leases, wills, letters patent and inquisitions - mainly to support his litigation in the first decades of the seventeenth century.[88] Battling for his Protestant identity in an overwhelmingly Catholic city, Edmund felt beleaguered and harassed at every turn among his fellow-patricians. Despite their 'combination and malice' against him, however, and notwithstanding his sense of being used, Sexton played a full part in municipal life, serving as mayor on four occasions, thus helping to save the corporation from censure or dissolution.[89] His greatest achievement, in his own view, was the fending off of many challenges to the liberties and rights of the two former monastic estates, the priory of St Mary and the Franciscan friary.[90]

---

[83] N. M. A. J., ix (1962-3), p. 15.

[84] O Fionnagáin, The Jesuit missions to Ireland, pp 18-19, 45.

[85] Dowd, History of Limerick, p. 91.

[86] W.B. Honey, 'Limerick Delftware' in N. M. A. J., iii (1942), pp 185-6

[87] For an introduction, see A.P.W. Malcolmson, 'Speaker Pery and the Pery papers' in N. M. A. J., xvi (1973-4), pp 33-9.

[88] For a catalogue of the documents that he considered of vital importance, see 'Papers relating to the Sexton family' (B.L., Add. MS 19865), p. 127.

[89] Limerick MSS (N.L.I., PC 875-9), 15/ 35.

[90] See note 16, above.

With royal approval, he asserted his claim to full enjoyment of these rich possessions which he conserved for his numerous progeny.[91]

It did not work out quite as Edmund Sexton would have anticipated. Due to a series of premature deaths among his seventeen children and the failure of his eventual heir to carry on the Sexton line, succession to the vast family fortune fell to one Edmund Pery.[92] He was the son of William, a recently-settled Englishman and Susanna Sexton, the sister of Edmund Sexton junior.[93] Edmund Pery had married into the prosperous Limerick patrician family of Stackpole and was resident at Stackpole court outside the city.[94] Thus there was a convergence of the rich landholding of the Stackpole and Sexton families in and around Limerick in the Pery name, and the sons of Edmund - Sexton and Stackpole - bear witness to this. Reverend Stackpole Pery produced two sons, Edmund Sexton Pery, the prominent politician and leading developer of eighteenth-century Limerick, and William Cecil Pery who was bishop of Limerick, and whose son, Edmund Henry Pery, became the first earl of Limerick.[95]

The abbey lands which had formed the basis of this patrimony played a key role in shaping the new physiognomy of Limerick in the eighteenth century. Firstly a prominent place was accorded the Perys in civic politics through their assiduous claim to their entitlement to a 'double voice' in the election of mayors and sheriffs. This was a direct inheritance from the priors of St Mary in the middle ages who enjoyed such a privilege, and the Sexton Pery papers contain much documentation justifying its continuation.[96] The double voting issue had been contested in 1679 when a mayoral election had been deadlocked by Edmund Pery's upholding of his right, and a favourable outcome for the family enabled them to vote twice in council elections until the 1730s when Stackpole Pery resorted to law to defend it.[97] By the time the privilege was abrogated in the mid-century Edmund Sexton Pery's political career had moved well beyond the municipal sphere. Perhaps less realistic were the family's claims to salmon from Lax weir and tallow from butchers in St John's parish in succession to the priors of St Mary's, but they also pursued these claims at law all the same. Jealous assertions of the original grant to

---

[91] See Limerick MSS (N.L.I., PC 875-9), 28/1.

[92] For Edmund's detailing of his children's births and deaths, see 'Sexton's notebook', c. 1635 (N.L.I., MS 16085), pp 143-4.

[93] Kevin Hannan, 'The rich inheritance of a Limerick mayor' in Lee (ed.), Remembering Limerick, pp 111-12.

[94] See, for example, Limerick MSS (N.L.I., PC 875-9), 15/49, 55, 56.

[95] Burke's peerage and baronetage (London, 1853 edn.), p. 615; see Figure 3, below.

[96] For eighteenth-century rehearsals of the history of the privilege of double voting, see, for example, Limerick MSS (N.L.I., PC 875-9),15/71, 74, 78; 21/1; 25/32; see also Irwin, 'Seventeenth-century Limerick', in Lee (ed.), Remembering Limerick, p. 120.

[97] See Malcolmson, 'Speaker Pery and the Pery papers' in N. M. A. J., xvi (1973-4), pp 33-9.

Edmund Sexton, based on meticulous record-keeping over two hundred years, served the interests of Pery municipal legitimacy very well.

Secondly, the monastic legacy gave the Sexton Perys an autonomous bailiwick outside the walls of Limerick to the north-east and the south-west. In his jousts with the corporation in the Jacobean period, Edmund Sexton junior had the grants confirmed by letters patent and got official recognition of the exclusion of these properties from the jurisdiction of the newly-created borough of Limerick.[98] Ironically, in view of Sexton's campaign to keep his lands free of priests and fugitives, one hundred years later the former St Francis abbey estate was reputed to be an asylum for papists under the auspices of the Perys. Stackpole Pery was forced to answer corporation claims before a house of lords enquiry that he was systematically engaged in harbouring and encouraging Catholics.[99] In his rebuttal he claimed that there were only twenty-six papists with holdings in the abbey as opposed to sixty-three Protestants: by contrast the corporation had forty Catholic residents as against three Protestants in its own suburb of Little Island. Pery denied that he had colluded in the establishment of a mass-house in the abbey estate, and offered to make it over for Protestant worship.[100] A contemporary rental of the St Francis abbey suburb shows that Catholic merchant families did indeed have substantial holdings there: these included John Creagh, James White and Patrick Stritch.[101] Stackpole Pery defended the community of St Francis abbey by asserting that they had always borne their share of quartering troops, despite the corporation's having no jurisdiction over them.[102]

A third way in which the medieval monastic legacy was conveyed to the eighteenth-century city was in the appointing of the estate of St Mary's priory called South Priors Land as the prime development site for the New Town of Limerick. Newtown Pery, as it came to be known after its landlord and developer, Edmund Sexton Pery, was a grid-planned suburb, which took shape on a green-field site along the Shannon bank.[103] It became the hub of Limerick's burgeoning commercial and residential expansion in the late eighteenth century. Among the mercantile community which set up businesses in the new precinct were several prominent Catholic families which had already come under the patronage of the Perys.[104]

---

[98] See Limerick MSS (N.L.I., PC 875-9), 28/1.

[99] Limerick MSS (N.L.I., PC 875-9), 15/73-8.

[100] Ibid., 15/74, 75.

[101] Ibid., 15/38.

[102] Ibid., 15/75.

[103] On the development of Newtown Pery, see Hill, Building of Limerick, pp 90-141; David Dickson, 'Large-scale developers and the growth of eighteenth-century Irish cities' in P. Butel and L.M. Cullen (ed.), Cities and merchants: French and Irish perspectives on urban development, 1500-1900 (Dublin, 1986), pp 117-18.

[104] See Hill, Building of Limerick, p 79; O'Connor, Exploring Limerick's past, p. 41.

Even during the most intensive application of the penal laws after 1704 there were Catholic merchants flourishing to the extent that they were taking on Protestant apprentices (a practice which was condemned by the Roman clergy).[105] This old urban interest formed a vociferous lobby which protested at commercial disabilities such as disproportionate cocket levies and billeting practices, enlisting the support of the most influential Limerick politician of his generation, Edmund Sexton Pery, who became speaker of the Irish parliament.[106] He supported the incorporation of the St Francis mercantile community within the mainstream of civic economic life, and his brother, William, later bishop of Limerick, aided the acquisition by Philip Roche of leases to lands in the Mardyke district which as a Catholic he was debarred from purchasing.[107] Roche was to the fore in developing Dominick Street, Bank Place and Rutland's Street, and a large granary on St Michael's Street, the original Roche's Store. Later the Roches acquired a house in George's Street in Newtown Pery for their bank.[108] Patrick and Thomas Arthur were among the first merchants to avail of the spacious quarters being developed outside the old walls. They invested in the building of Arthur's Quay, constructing a terrace facing the river, and they also built terraces upon what became known as Patrick Street and Francis Street.[109] Martin Creagh, another Catholic merchant, leased land for building on Bedford Row in Newtown Pery.[110]

Ironically, then, in view of the contentions over the Sextons' patrimony in the 1550s, it was under its awning that the descendants of the family's rivals regained a foothold on the expanding grounds of Limerick's commerce and society two hundred years later. The cherished monastic privilege of double voting had brought its Sexton and Pery holders to a position of dominance in municipal life which bred political liberalism. The Sexton estate of St Francis abbey was the locus for the regrouping of many of the older burgher families during the period of exclusion, especially after 1700. And the legacy of St Mary's priory, South Priors land, became the fashionable new urban frontier which the old families played a full part in developing.

Counterfactualism has had a vogue among historians of late. So what if the older borough elites in Ireland had adopted the Reformation in the sixteenth century? Perhaps the progress of the Sextons, the only Protestant Irish family of note in

---

[105] White's annals' (N.L.I., MS 2714), pp 176-7

[106] For the political background, see Eamon O'Flaherty, 'Urban politics and municipal reform in Limerick, 1723-62' in Eighteenth-century Ireland, vi (1991), pp 105-120.

[107] Lenihan, Limerick, pp 398-9.

[108] Hill, Building of Limerick, pp 96-7, 113.

[109] Ibid., pp 96-100.

[110] Ibid., p. 110.

Limerick, adumbrates an answer. But, clinging to actuality, it may be possible to posit the thesis that the older civic patriciates of Limerick and elsewhere had a more abiding role to play in the formation of modern Ireland than is conventionally thought. The challenges of the political and religious upheavals of the seventeenth century tempered the qualities of resilience and adaptability of these families, at least in the case of Limerick. Wise in the ways of the municipal maelstrom and confident in their history and heritage, they were positioned to respond imaginatively to opportunities when they opened up in the eighteenth century. A leading member of the Catholic committee in the 1790s referred to the 'corporation spirit' which the experience of adversity had bred among Catholics.[111] Rather than interpreting this term in a narrow sense, it may be warranted to understand by it the accumulated store of sagacity and sophistication which came from generations of civic living.

---

[111] Cited in Maureen Wall, 'The rise of a Catholic middle class in eighteenth-century Ireland' in Irish Historical Studies, xi (1958), p. 113.

Named in 1609 charter	Aldermen in 1643	Aldermen in 1687
Arthur, William	Arthur, Thomas	Arthur, Nicholas
Bonvile, Robert	Bourke, James	Bourke, Sir Oliver
Bourke, William	Creagh, John	Craven, James
Comyn, David	Creagh, Peter (Piers)	Craven, William
Creagh, William	Creagh, William	Creagh FitzPierse, James
Everard, Patrick	Cusack, Andrew	Creagh, Michael
Fanning, Clement	Fanning, Francis	Creagh, Stephen
Fox, Edmund	Fleming, Nicholas	Ford, John
Galway, James	Fox, James	Galway, Sir James
Gould, Patrick	Fox, Nicholas	Hannan, Robert
Gromwell, James	Hackett, James	Harrold, Thomas
Harrold, George	Nihill, Daniel	King, Sir William
Leo, Edmund	O'Haghy, William	Lacy, Pierce
Loftus, John	Power, Thomas	Leonard, John
Long, William	Roche, William	McNamara, John
Loys, Robert	Stritch, Luke	Power, Thomas
Meagh, William	Stritch, William	Rice FitzEdward, John
Mulroney, Thomas	White, David	Rice FitzWilliam, John
Power, Thomas	White, Dominic	Roche, Dominic
Rice, David	White, James	Roche, Thomas
Roche, Stephen	White, Thomas	Rouzel, J. Baptist
Rochford, Robert	Woulfe, George	Smith, Robert
Sexton, Edmund		Taverner, James
Skeolan, John		Warr, Edward
Stackpole, Peter		
Stritch, John		
Walter, Michael		
White, David		
Verdon, William		
Wolfe, Thomas		

Figure 1: Lists of senior city councillors of Limerick in the seventeenth century, showing the continuity of family names throughout the period.

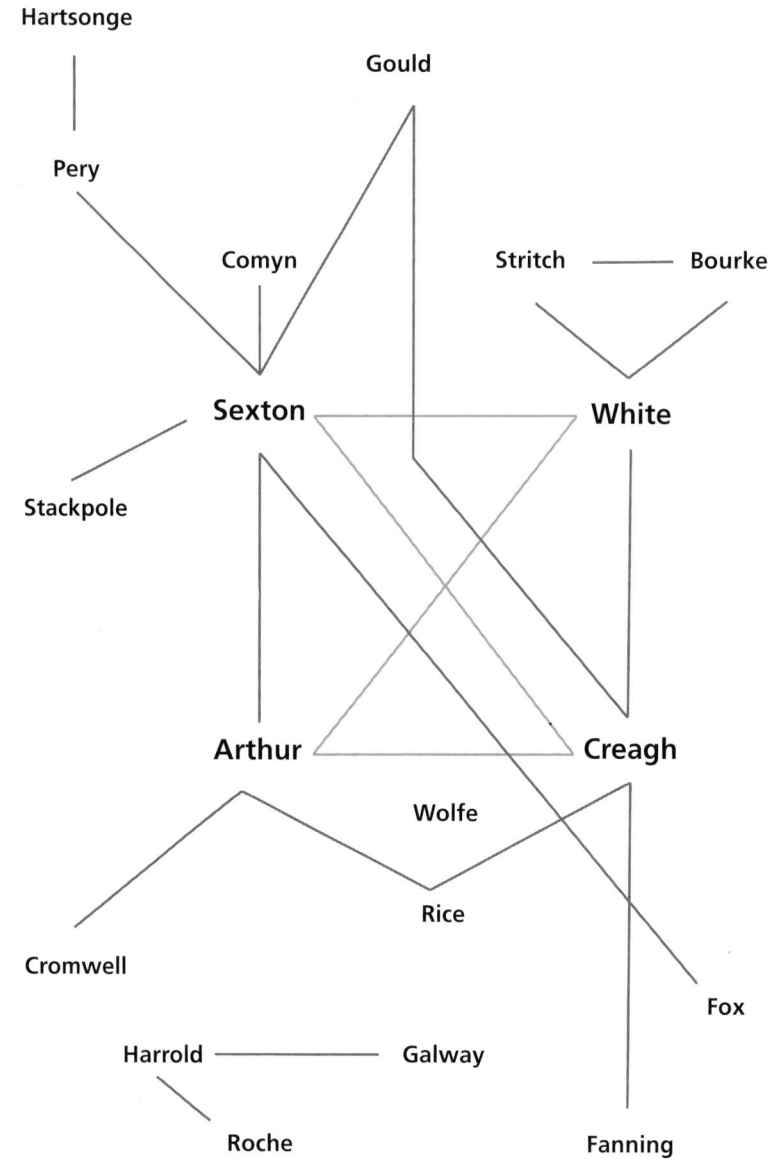

Figure 2: Pattern of marriage alliances between leading Limerick patrician families, linked to the four core families of Sexton, White, Arthur and Creagh.

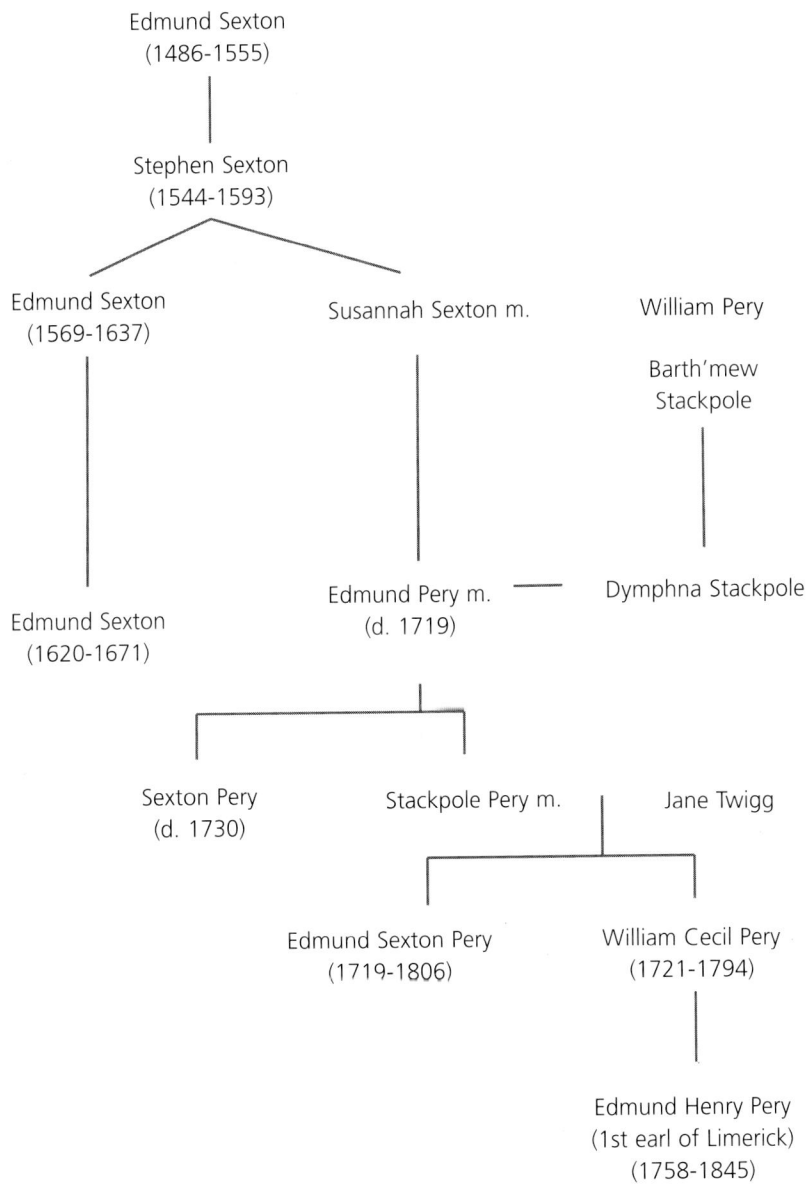

Figure 3: Descent of the family of Sexton Pery of Limerick, late medieval period to the nineteenth century

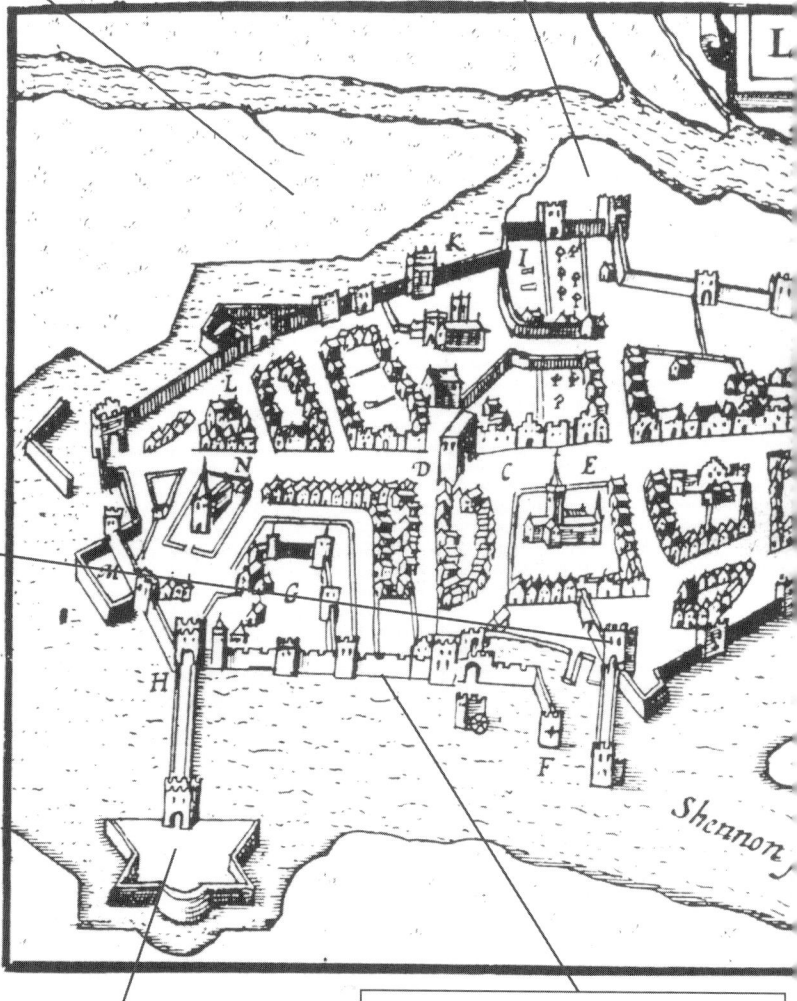

Hunc pontem ac viam stratam fieri fecit Petrus Creagh filius Andreae major civitatis Limericensis sumptis ejudem civitatis 1635

SANCTE JACOBE
DEFENDE NOS AB HOSTE
HIC BELLONA TONAT SEDET HIC ASTREA RENASCENS
HAC PIETAS AD AQUAS, AC SACRA PANDITITER
ANNO DOMINI MDC XL VII
R.R. CAROLI DOMINIC FANNING PRAETORE
DAVID CREAGH ET JACOBO SEXTON VICEC

CAROLO REGE REGNANTE PETRO CREAGH PRAETORE ANNO DNI MDC. XLII

This paving was only ended at the charges of the Corporation, James White FitzJames esquir Being Mayor ANNO DI MDCXXXVIII

Haec Moenia reparavit expensis Publicis Dominius Gulielmus Comyn Armiger hujus Familiae et Cognominis Vicessimus Praetor Civitatis Lymericensis. Anno Domini MDCXLI

Map of Limerick (1611) showing approximate location of seventeenth-century plaques commemorating patrician donors

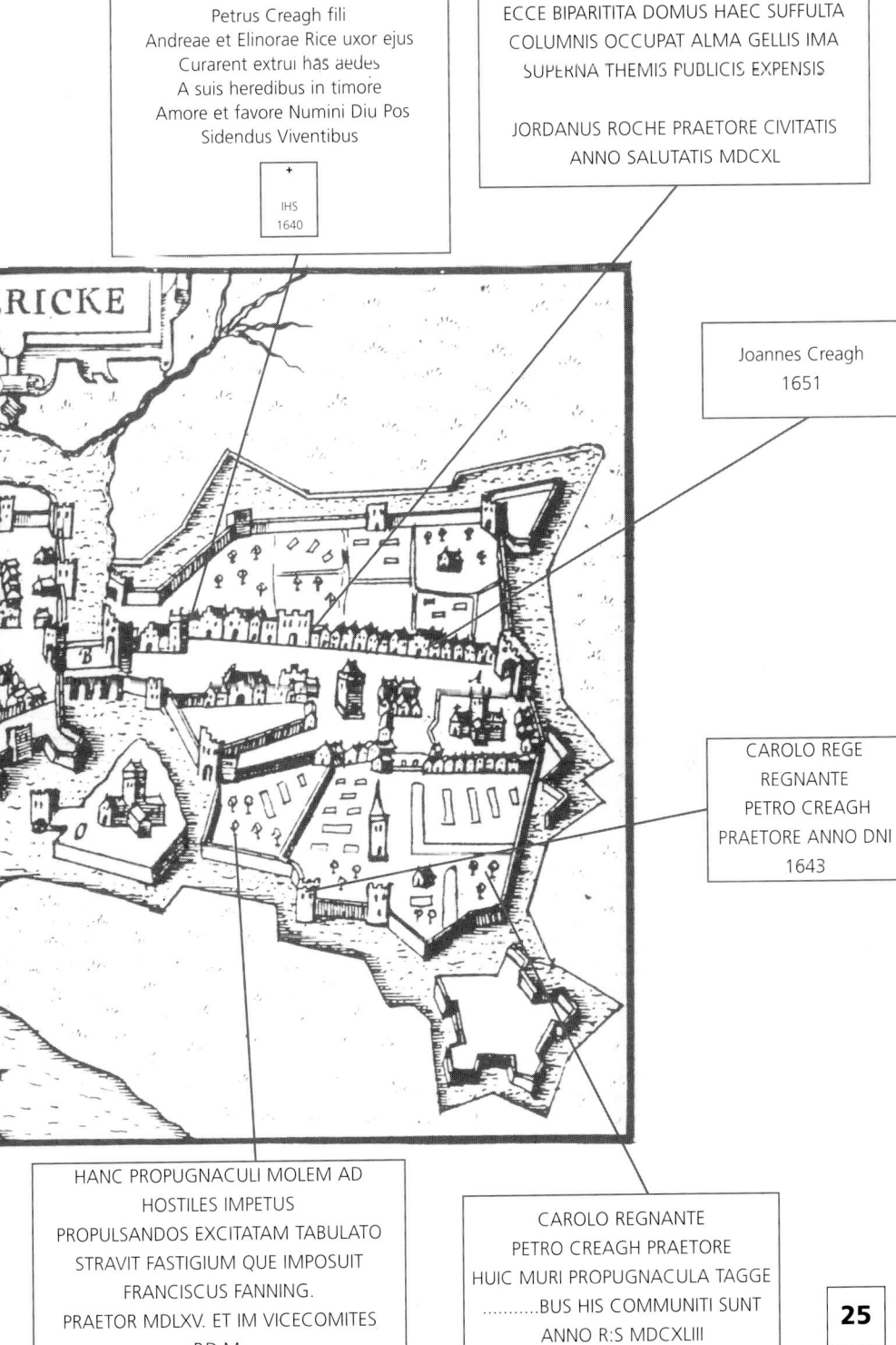

O'DONNELL LECTURES
Publications in the series

1957   I   "The O'Neills in Spain"
by Micheline Walsh

1958   II   "Justin MacCarthy, Lord Mountcashel"
by John A. Murphy, MA

1958   III   "Daniel O'Connor Sligo: His Family and His Times"
by Sir Charles Petrie

1960   IV   "The MacDonnells of Antrim on the Continent"
by Micheline Walsh

1961   V   "Thomas Francis Meagher",
by Professor Denis Gwynn   **(out of print)**

1962   VI   "Napper Tandy and the European Crisis of 1798-1803"
by Síle Ní Chinnéide

1963   VII   "Charles Gavan Duffy and the Repeal Movement"
by Kevin B. Nowlan, MA, PhD

1964   VIII   "Waterford Merchants Abroad"
by Seamus Pender

1965   IX   "Captain Myles Walter Keogh, United States Army 1840-1876"
by G.A. Hayes-McCoy, MA, PhD, DLitt, MRIA

1966   X   "Toirdbleach Ó Conchubair (1088-1156), King of Connacht, King of Ireland, Co. Freasabra",
by Rev. Professor John G. Ryan

1967   XI   "The Study of Family History in Ireland"
by Professor John G. Barry

1968   XII   "The Influence of the Irish on the Catholic Church in America in the 19th Century"
by Patrick K. Egan, PP, PhD

1969   XIII   "The Rise of Uí Néill and the High-kingship of Ireland"
by Professor John Byrne

1970   XIV   "The Nineteenth Century Novel and Irish Social History; Some Aspects"
by Professor O. McDonagh

	XV		**Not Published**
1972	**XVI**	"Irish Families: The Archival Aspects" by R. Dudley Edwards	
	XVII		**Not Published**
1974	**XVIII**	"The Formation of the Old English Elite in Ireland" by Nicholas P. Canny	**(out of print)**
1975	**XIX**	"No Hero in the House; Diarmait MacMurchada and the coming of the Normans to Ireland" by F.X. Martin, OSA	
1976	**XX**	"Land, Law and Society in 16th Century Ireland" by K.W. Nicholls	
1977	**XXI**	"Thomas Drummond and the Government of Ireland 1835-41" by M.A.G. Ó Tuathaigh	
1979	**XXII**	"Democracy and its 19th Century Irish Critics" by Donal McCartney, MA, PhD	
1979	**XXIII**	"The Catholic Middle Classes in Pre-Famine Cork" by John B. O'Brien, MA, PhD	
1981	**XXIV**	"Irish Population before Petty, Problems and Possibilities" by Gearóid MacNiocaill	
1983	**XXV**	"The Four Leaved Shamrock, Electoral Politics and the National Imagination in Independent Ireland" by Dr Ronan Fanning	
1984	**XXVI**	"Maria Edgeworth and the Colonial Mind" by Tom Dunne, PhD	
1986	**XXVII**	"The Pale and the Far North *Government and Society in two early Tudor Borderlands*" by Steven G. Ellis	

Copies of these lectures may be obtained from:
The Registrar, National University of Ireland, 49 Merrion Square, Dublin 2
Tel: (353 1) 676 7246; **Fax:** (353 1) 661 9665; **Email:** registrar@nui.ie

Price per copy: £2 including postage and packaging